Doctor Mozart Music Theory Workbook
Answers for Level 1 and Older Beginners

Level 1A

Level 1B

Level 1C

Older Beginners

1A

1B

1C

OB

Version 1.1.0

Doctor Mozart Music Theory Workbook, Answers for Level 1 & OB.   © MMVI, MMXVII Machiko and Paul Christopher Musgrave.   Published by April Avenue Music.   www.DoctorMozart.com

For Parents and Teachers

This answer book is intended to make marking and correcting easier for you. It matches the current versions of the Doctor Mozart Level 1 and Older Beginners workbooks. It contains all of the answers, except where the exercise is mainly creative, and there is no single correct answer.

The actual Doctor Mozart workbooks are printed in color, which of course appeals to children. In contrast, this answer book is printed in black and white, to make it more affordable.

We hope you find this answer book helpful.

Thank you for choosing Doctor Mozart.

Doctor Mozart Music Theory Workbook, Answers for Level 1 & OB. © MMVI, MMXVII Machiko and Paul Christopher Musgrave.   Published by April Avenue Music.   www.DoctorMozart.com

Doctor Mozart® Music Theory Workbook Level 1A

In-Depth Piano Theory Fun for Children's Music Lessons and Home Schooling

1
A

We will help you remember each lesson.

Learning theory will help you play music better.

Level 1A- Contents

Hi! I'm Doctor Mozart.

Highly Effective for Beginners Learning a Musical Instrument.

Doctor Mozart workbooks are filled with friendly cartoon characters. They make it fun to learn music theory in-depth. And in-depth music theory knowledge is essential for children learning a musical instrument. Use Doctor Mozart workbooks by themselves or with other teaching materials. Use them for music lessons and for home schooling.

The authors, Machiko and Paul Musgrave, are both graduates of Juilliard. Machiko has taught piano and theory at Soai University in Japan. Paul is an Associate of the Royal Conservatory of Music. The authors hope you enjoy using this book!

Many thanks to Kevin Musgrave for his meticulous proof-reading and insightful suggestions.
Created by Machiko and Paul Christopher Musgrave. Illustrated by Machiko Yamane Musgrave.

1.1.2

Doctor Mozart Music Theory Workbook, Answers for Level 1 & OB. © MMVI, MMXVII Machiko and Paul Christopher Musgrave.   Published by April Avenue Music.   www.DoctorMozart.com

Meet the Keyboard

Look at this keyboard. Do you see groups of black keys?

Circle all the groups of 3 black keys.

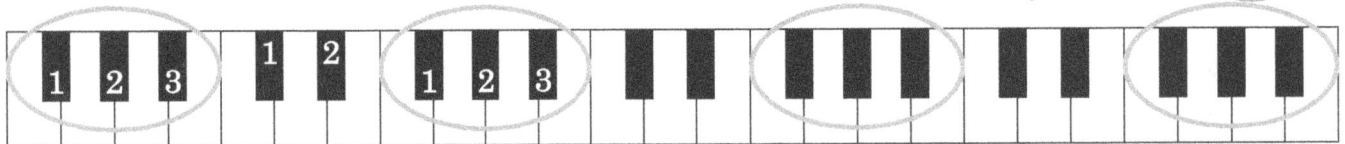

The black keys are always in groups of 2 and 3. Circle any mistakes on these keyboards.

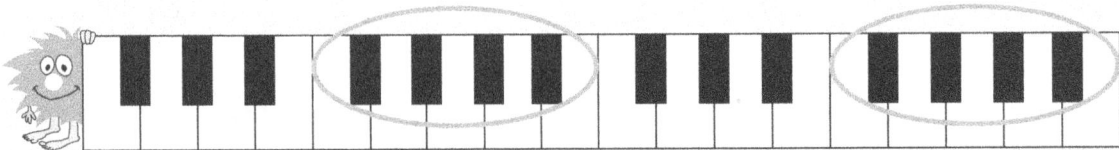

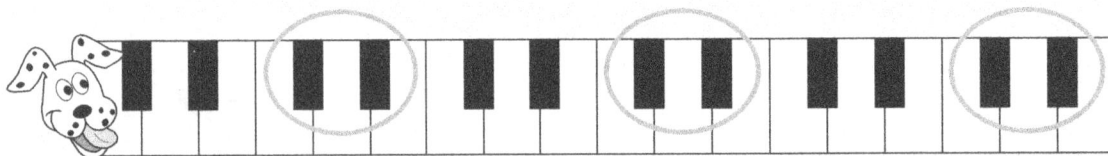

Write a check mark in the box beside each correct answer.

Black keys should be in groups of		The order of the groups should be	
2 and 4	☐	3 2 2 3	☐
3 and 4	☐	2 3 5 2	☐
2 and 3	✓	2 3 2 3	✓
5 and 3	☐	any order is fine.	☐

Doctor Mozart Music Theory Workbook, Answers for Level 1 & OB. © MMVI, MMXVII Machiko and Paul Christopher Musgrave.   Published by April Avenue Music.   www.DoctorMozart.com

The Music Alphabet

Circle all the Ds on this keyboard. Is there any key named H? __No__

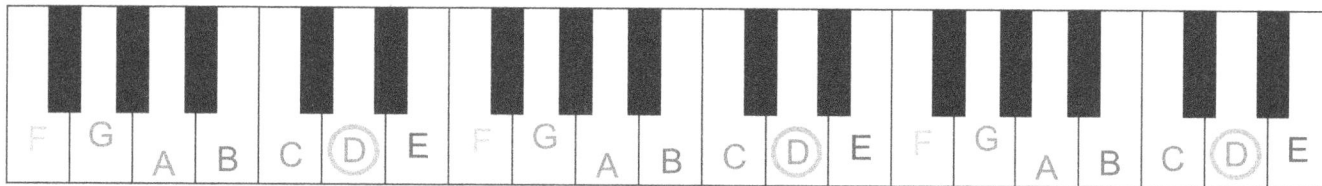

This is the lower end of the keyboard.

This is the higher end.

How many alphabet letters have I written on this board? __7__

A B C D E F G

What 7 alphabet letters are used for piano keys?

__A B C D E F G__

Dean is playing a key named D. Trace the D. Is it inside a group of 2 black keys? __Yes__

Trace the letter D.

D is a white key. It is colored blue on this page to help you see it.

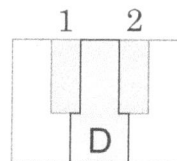

D

Trace the key.

Next, number the black keys. Start each group with a number 1.

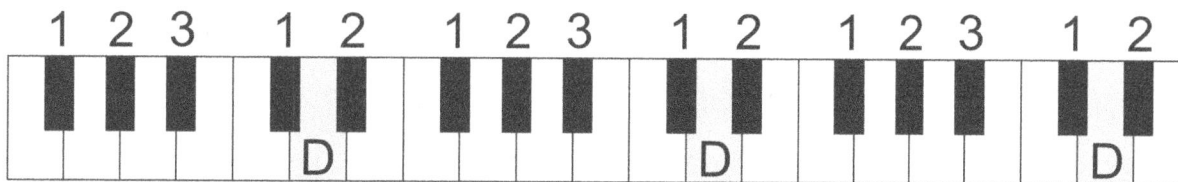

1 2 3   1 2   1 2 3   1 2   1 2 3   1 2

D   D   D

Name all the colored keys.

Here are 2 ways to write D.

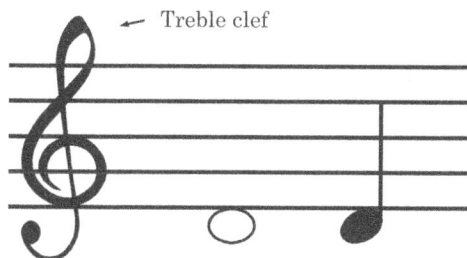

Treble clef

Trace or color the notes.

Doctor Mozart Music Theory Workbook, Answers for Level 1 & OB.   © MMVI, MMXVII Machiko and Paul Christopher Musgrave.   Published by April Avenue Music.   www.DoctorMozart.com

D's Two Neighbors

What key is the cat playing? __C__ Is it near a group of 2 black keys? __Yes__

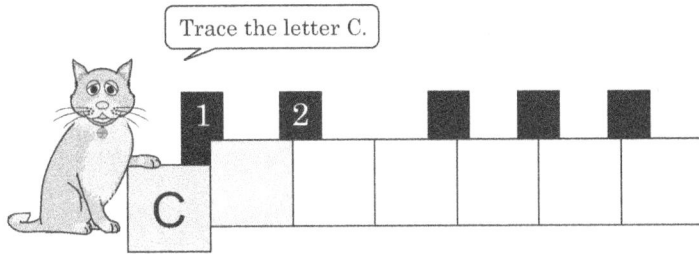

Trace the letter C.

Trace it.

Trace the key.

C is to the *left* of D.

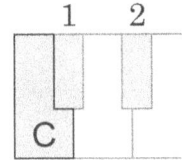

Next, number the black keys. Name every C and D.

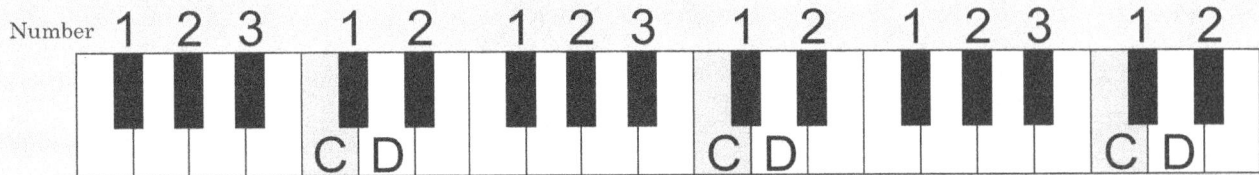

Number 1 2 3 1 2 1 2 3 1 2 1 2 3 1 2

C D   C D   C D

How many Cs are there on this keyboard? __3__

Ethan has found a key. It is named __E__.

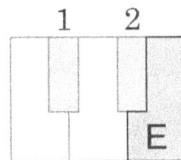

Trace the letter E.

Trace the key.

D is between C and E.

Number the black keys. Name every C, D, and E.

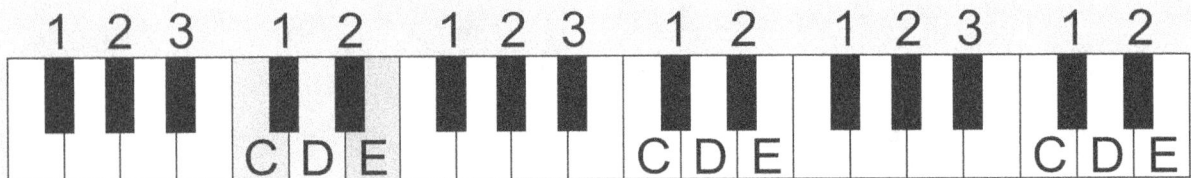

1 2 3 1 2 1 2 3 1 2 1 2 3 1 2

C D E   C D E   C D E

Lower notes   Higher notes

How many Es are there on this keyboard? __3__

CDE Quiz

Name all the Ds.

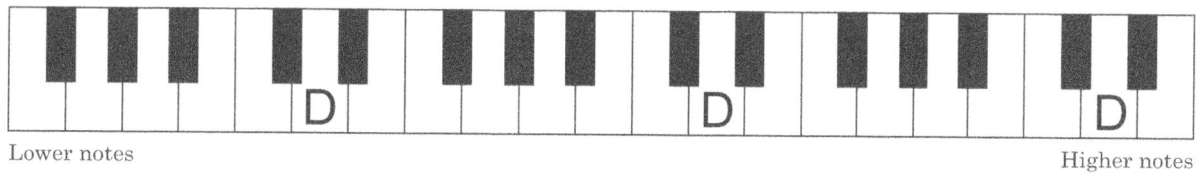

1 A

D is between C and E.

Lower notes   D   D   D   Higher notes

Name all the Cs and Es.

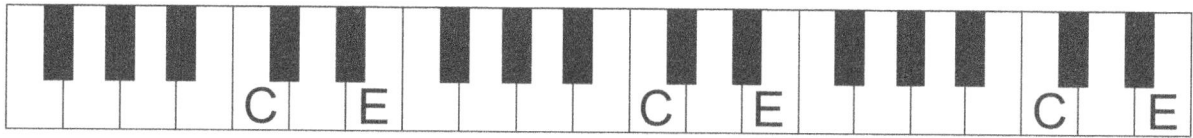

C   E   C   E   C   E

Name them.

Name all the Cs, Ds and Es. How many Ds are there? __3__

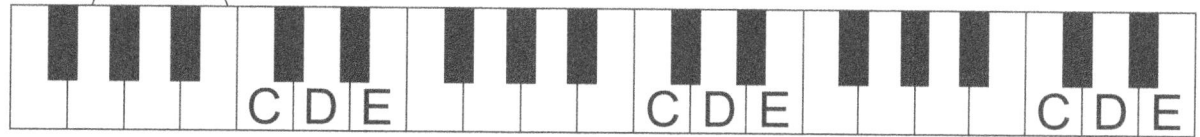

C D E   C D E   C D E

Name the colored keys.

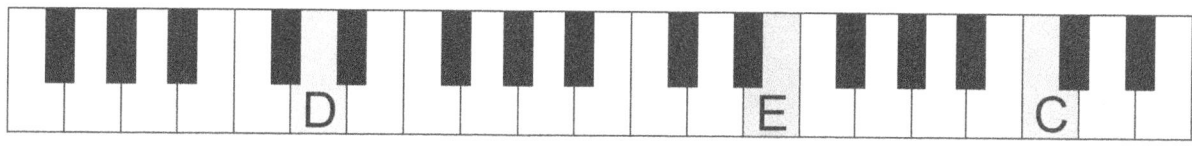

D   E   C

Here are 4 ways to write C.   Here are 2 ways to write E.

Trace or color the notes.

Bass clef

Treble clef

You will learn more about writing notes later in this book.

Doctor Mozart Music Theory Workbook, Answers for Level 1 & OB.   © MMVI, MMXVII Machiko and Paul Christopher Musgrave.   Published by April Avenue Music.   www.DoctorMozart.com

Beside the 3 Black Keys

Fiona has found a key. It is named __F__. Is it near a group of 3 black keys? __Yes__

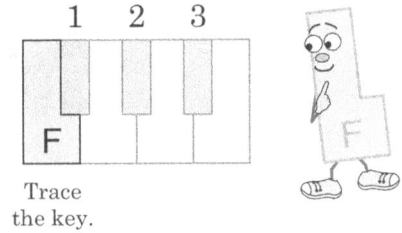

Trace the letter F.

Trace the key.

F is on the *left* side of the 3 black keys.

F is on the ___left___ side of the 3 black keys.

Number the black keys. Name all the Fs.

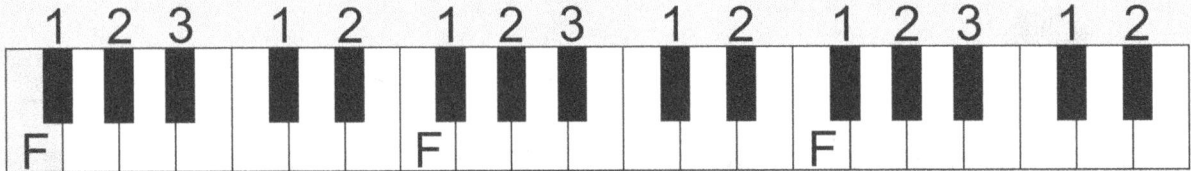

How many Fs did you find? __3__

Now the bee has found a key. It is named __B__. Is it near a group of 3 black keys? __Yes__

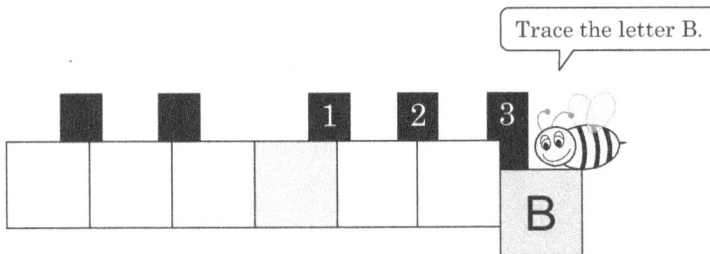

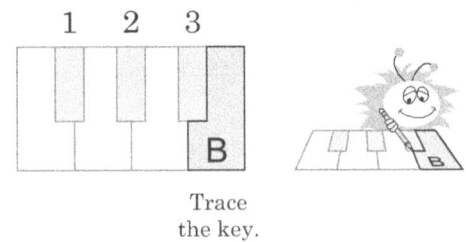

Trace the letter B.

Trace the key.

B is on the *right* side of the 3 black keys.

B is on the ___right___ side of the 3 black keys.

Name all the Fs and Bs on the keyboard.

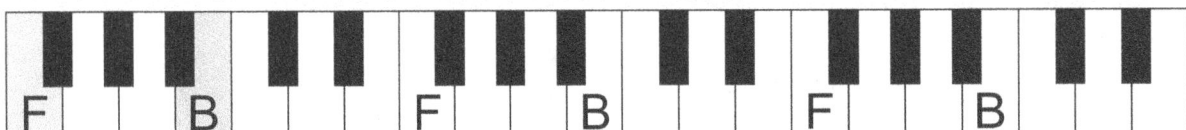

Where are G and A?

Gina has found a key named _G_. Is it inside a group of 3 black keys? __Yes__

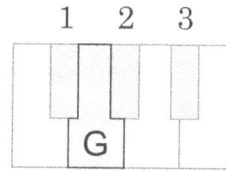

Trace
the key.

Name all the Gs on the keyboard.

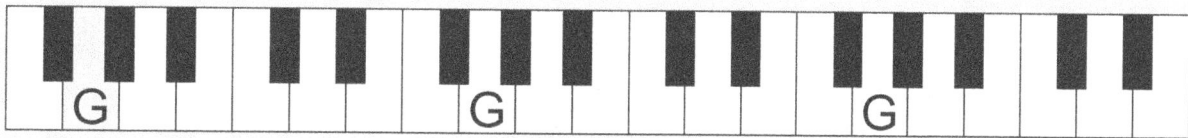

This alien has found a key named _A_.
Is it inside a group of 3 black keys? __Yes__

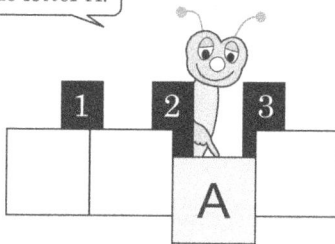

A is between the 2nd and 3rd black keys.
A is between the 2nd and _3rd_ black keys.

What 2 notes are
within every group
of 3 black keys?

_G_ and _A_

Name all the Gs and As on the keyboard.

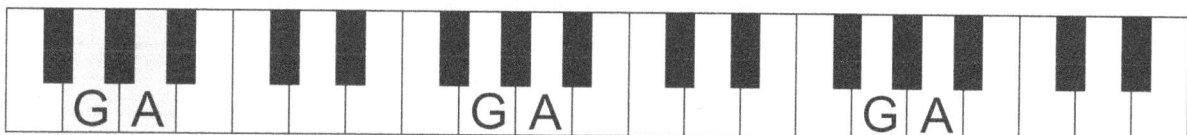

Doctor Mozart Music Theory Workbook, Answers for Level 1 & OB.   © MMVI, MMXVII Machiko and Paul Christopher Musgrave.   Published by April Avenue Music.   www.DoctorMozart.com

FGAB Quiz

Name all the Fs and Bs.

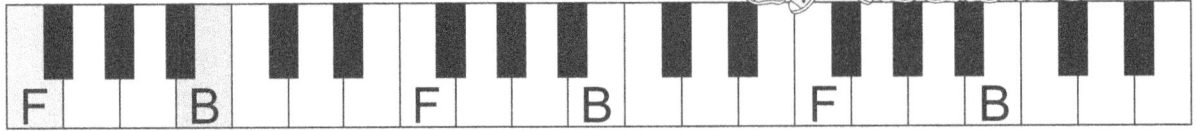

F   B   F   B   F   B

Name all the Gs and As.

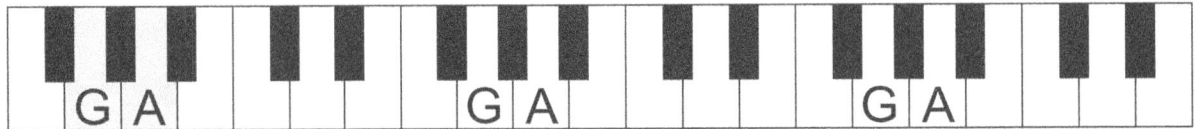

G A   G A   G A

Circle each group of 2 black keys. Name each F, G, A, and B.

F G A B   F G A B   F G A B

Name the colored keys.

G and A are within each group of 3 black keys.

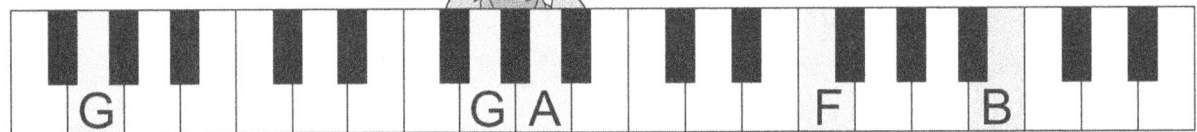

G   G A   F   B

Name all the white keys.

F G A B C D E F G A B C D E

Here are some ways to write F, G, A, and B.

Trace or color the notes.

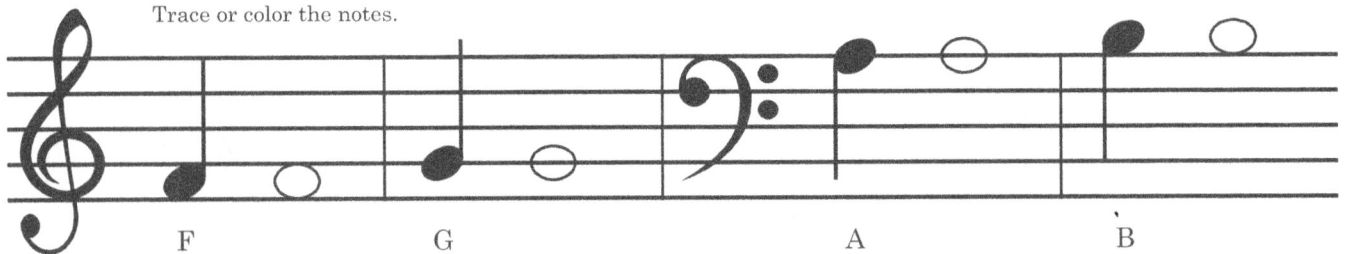

F   G   A   B

A Step or a Skip?

Circle the pairs of colored keys that are next-door neighbors.

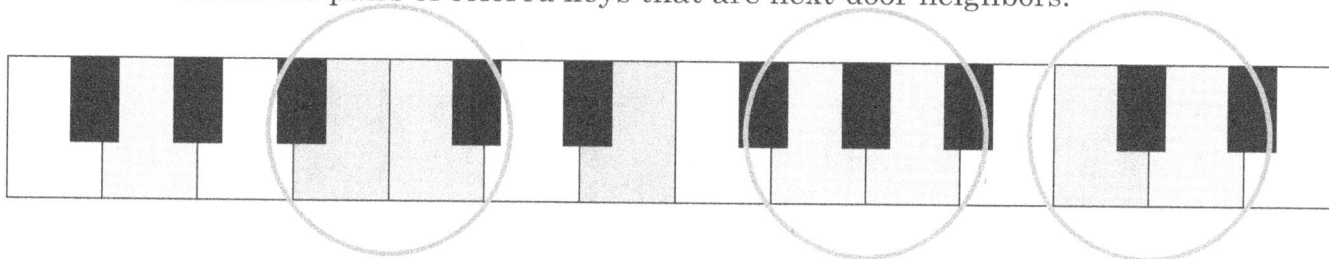

Trace the gray letters on the keyboard. Trace the brackets.

Are F and G neighbors? **Yes**
F and G make a step, because they are neighbors. Any two white keys that are neighbors make a **step**.

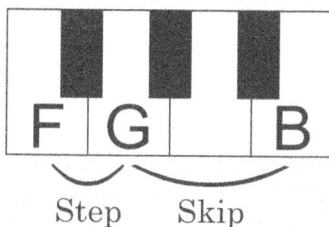

F G B

Step Skip

Are G and B neighbors? **No**.
G and B make a skip, because they are not neighbors. Any two white keys that are not neighbors make a **skip**.

Step

Skip

Write *Step* or *Skip* under each bracket.

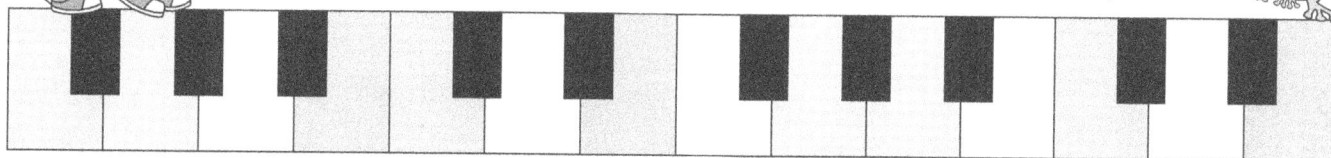

Step Skip Step Skip Skip Step Skip Skip

For each colored key, name the white keys that are one step higher, and one step lower.

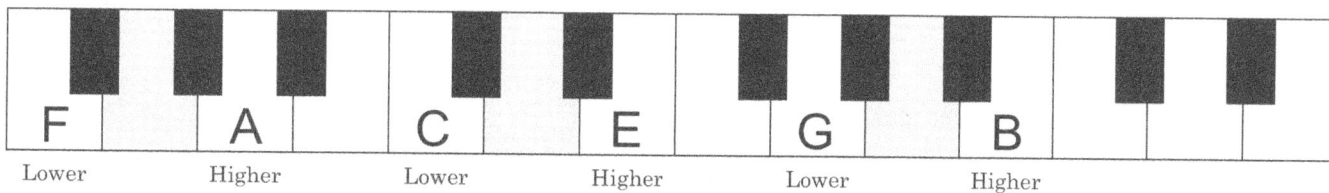

F A C E G B

Lower Higher Lower Higher Lower Higher

Name the colored keys. Mark the steps and skips.

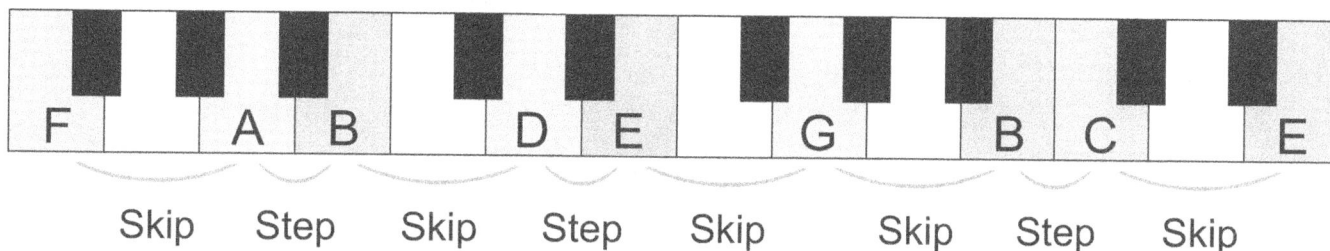

F A B D E G B C E

Skip Step Skip Step Skip Skip Step Skip

Step & Skip Quiz

For each colored key, name the white keys
that are one step higher and one step lower.

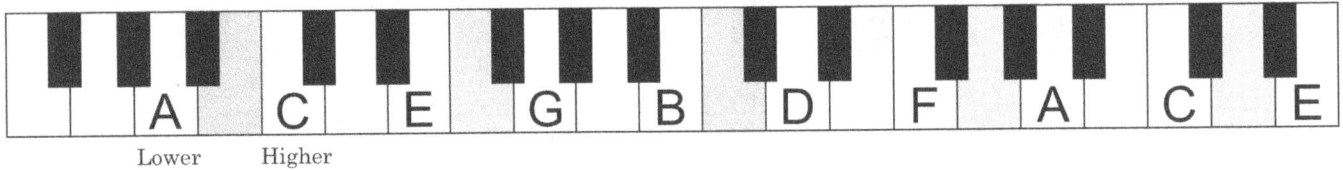

A C E G B D F A C E

Lower   Higher

Write a bracket under each skip. Ignore the steps.

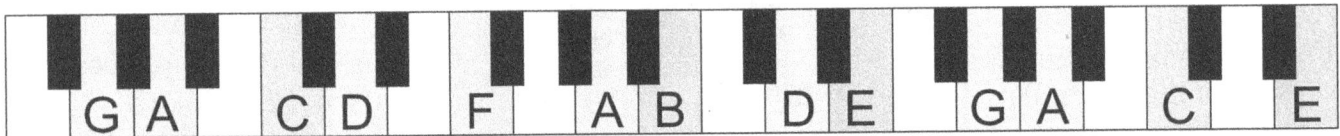

G A C D F A B D E G A C E

Name the
colored keys.

Name the white keys on either side of each gray key. Does each pair make a step? __Yes__

F G C D G A D E A B

Each of these steps and skips
is made with two white keys.
Name those keys.

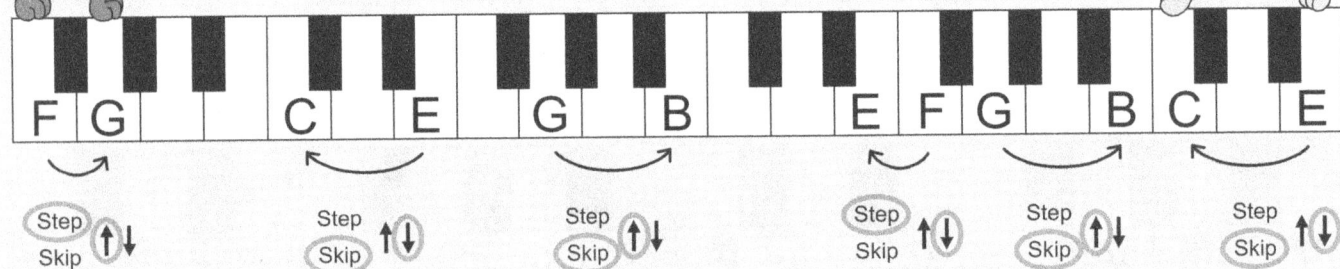

F G C E G B E F G B C E

Step ↑↓ Step ↑↓ Step ↑↓ Step ↑↓ Step ↑↓ Step ↑↓
Skip   Skip   Skip   Skip   Skip   Skip

Circle the correct words and arrows.

Circle each pair of letters
that makes a step:

(BC) CE (FG) FA BD (GA)

CE
BC
FA

Circle each pair of letters
that makes a skip:

(AC) GA CD EF (GB)(DF)

Doctor Mozart Music Theory Workbook, Answers for Level 1 & OB.   © MMVI, MMXVII Machiko and Paul Christopher Musgrave.   Published by April Avenue Music.   www.DoctorMozart.com

A Staff is Like a Ladder for Notes

Here are some birds on a ladder.

These birds are
higher on the ladder.
They sing higher.

These birds sing __higher__.

These birds are
lower on the ladder.
They sing lower.

These birds sing __lower__.

Trace the 5 gray lines. They make a staff.   How many lines are there in the staff? __5__

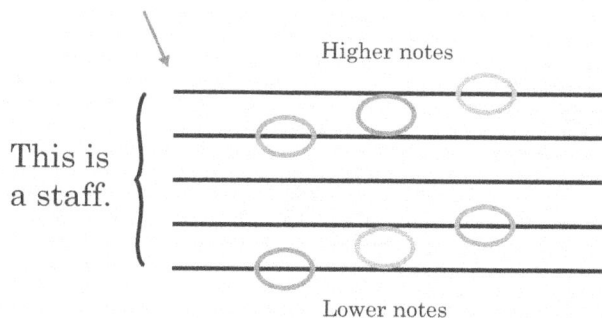

Higher notes

This is
a staff.

These notes sound _____higher_____.

These notes sound _____lower_____.

Lower notes

For each pair of notes,
write an H to show
which note is higher.

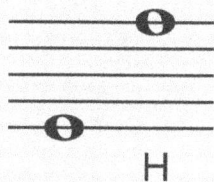

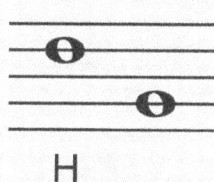

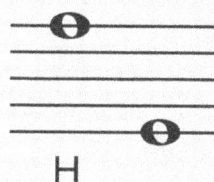

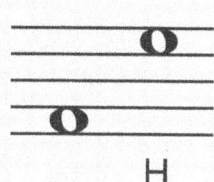

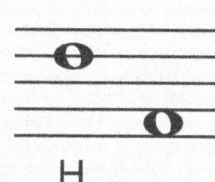

H   H   H   H   H

Trace the lines.
The lines go
through the
notes, so these
notes are called
line notes.

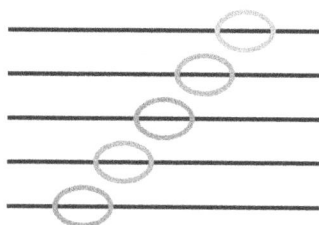

Trace the lines.
These notes are
in the spaces
between the
lines, so we call
these *space* notes.

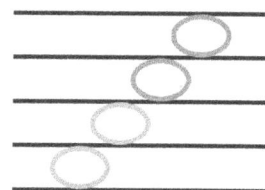

Doctor Mozart Music Theory Workbook, Answers for Level 1 & OB.   © MMVI, MMXVII Machiko and Paul Christopher Musgrave.   Published by April Avenue Music.   www.DoctorMozart.com

Let's Write Some Notes!

Trace this note.

Start at the top.

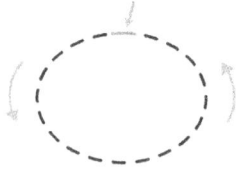

This shape is called an *oval*.

Trace these too.

Doctor Mozart is writing
a note with his roller blades!
Trace the note with your pencil.

Next, trace the numbers and the notes.

Are these line notes or
space notes? __line__ notes.

Are these line notes or
space notes? __space__ notes.

5
4
3
2
1

4
3
2
1

Are these notes going
up or down? __Up__

Are these notes going
up or down? __Down__

How many lines are there in the staff? __5__ How many spaces are there between the lines? __4__

Trace these notes. Fill in the blanks.

These are __line__ notes.

These are __space__ notes.

Are these notes going up or down? __Up__

Are these notes going up or down? __Down__

WHICH LINE? WHICH SPACE?

Trace these notes. Write the line number for each note.

| 5 | 4 | 2 | 3 | 4 | 2 | 1 | 3 | 2 |

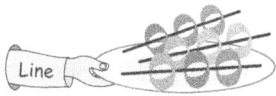

Next, write a line note to match the number in each box.

| 3 | 1 | 5 | 2 | 4 | 1 | 3 | 4 | 2 |

Trace these notes. Write the space number for each note.

| 3 | 4 | 2 | 3 | 1 | 3 | 2 | 4 | 1 |

Next, write a space note to match the number in each box.

| 3 | 1 | 4 | 2 | 1 | 4 | 3 | 1 | 2 |

STAFF CODE QUIZ

Write the correct note
above each box.

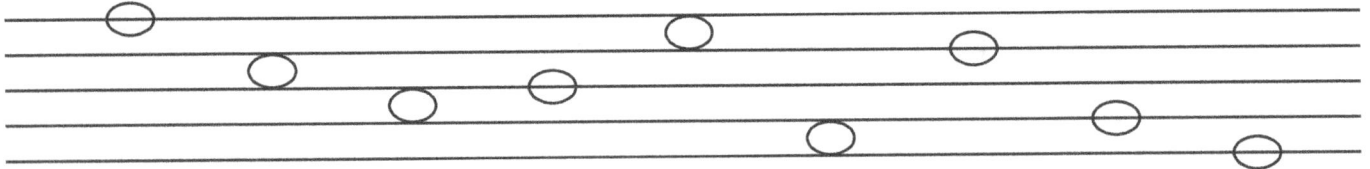

| 5L | 3S | 2S | 3L | 4S | 1S | 4L | 2L | 1L |

5th Line   **3rd Space**

Trace each note. Write its code in the box below it.

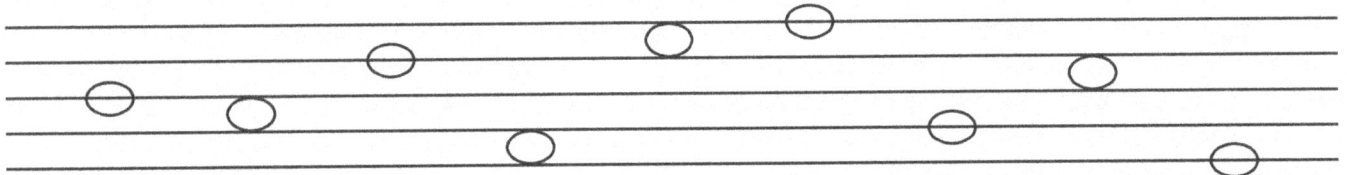

| 3L | 2S | 4L | 1S | 4S | 5L | 2L | 3S | 1L |

Circle the correct arrows to show whether the notes are going up or down.

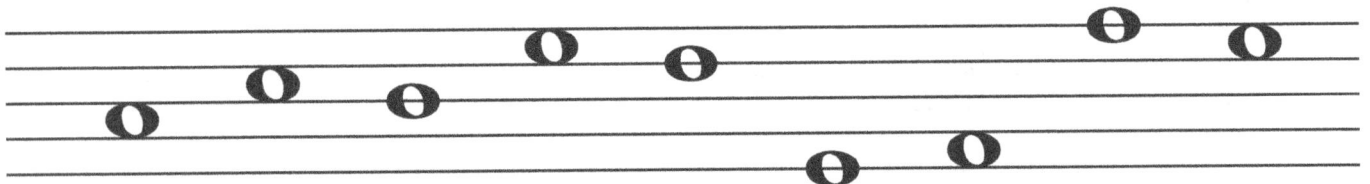

↓↑ ↓↑ ↓↑ ↓↑ ↓↑ ↓↑ ↓↑ ↓↑

 Up!    Down.

Write notes that go up or down.
Follow the direction of the arrows.

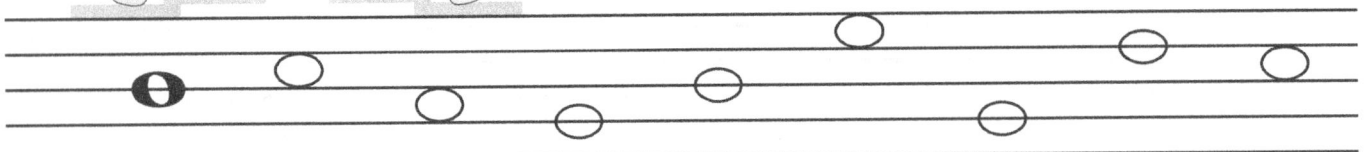

This is just one of many possible correct answers.

↑   ↓   ↓   ↑   ↑   ↓   ↑   ↓

Doctor Mozart Music Theory Workbook, Answers for Level 1 & OB.   © MMVI, MMXVII Machiko and Paul Christopher Musgrave.   Published by April Avenue Music.   www.DoctorMozart.com

Name the 2 notes shown by
each curved arrow.

Skip!

F G   C E   G B   D E   G A   C E

1
A

Step	Step	Step	Step	Step	Step
Skip ↑↓	Skip ↑↓	Skip ↑↓	Skip ↑↓	Skip ↑↓	Skip ↑↓

Circle the correct words and arrows.

Can you write steps and skips on the staff? Trace these notes and find out.

Leave out this note.   Leave out this note.

Step up   Skip up   Step down   Skip down

Below, circle the correct words and arrows.

Step	Step	Step	Step	Step	Step
Skip ↑↓	Skip ↑↓	Skip ↑↓	Skip ↑↓	Skip ↑↓	Skip ↑↓

Step

Skip

Write notes to match the words and arrows.

Step   Skip   Skip   Step   Skip   Step   Skip   Skip

↓   ↑   ↓   ↑   ↑   ↓   ↓   ↑

Doctor Mozart Music Theory Workbook, Answers for Level 1 & OB.   © MMVI, MMXVII Machiko and Paul Christopher Musgrave.   Published by April Avenue Music.   www.DoctorMozart.com

The Clefs: Bass and Treble

Here are two musical signs,
which we call clefs.

The bass clef is
for lower notes.

The treble clef is
for higher notes.

Trace the
brackets.

Low notes

High notes

Middle C is a special
note near the middle
of your keyboard.

The special C near the middle of your keyboard is called ___middle___ C.

The bass clef is for ___lower___ notes.   The treble clef is for ___higher___ notes.

Let's write some clefs.
Trace these treble clefs. Write 2 treble clefs by yourself.

Color the
G line green.

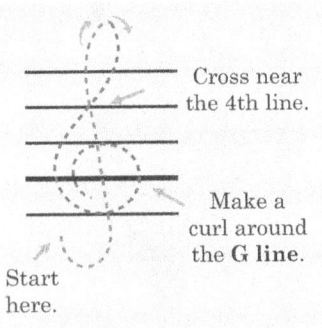

Cross near
the 4th line.

Make a
curl around
the **G line**.

Start
here.

Trace these bass clefs. Write 2 bass clefs by yourself.

Color the
F line yellow.

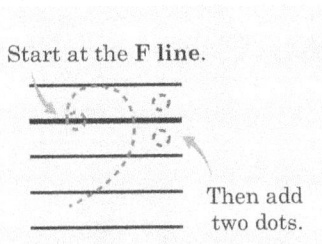

Start at the **F line**.

Then add
two dots.

CLEF and STAFF QUIZ

Trace these bass clefs.
Then write 3 bass clefs on your own.

Color the F line yellow.

Next, fill in the blanks.

__bass__ __clef__ ← Treble clef or bass clef?

__treble__ __clef__ ← Treble clef or bass clef?

C   C   C   C   C

Middle

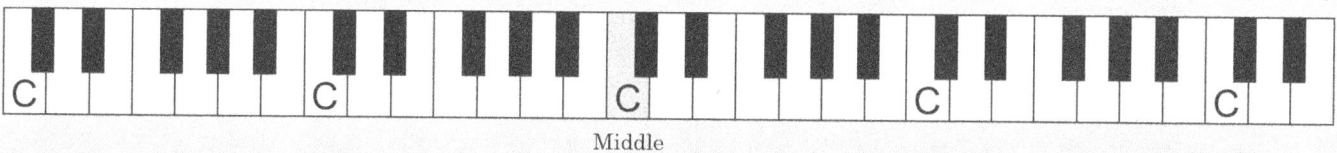

Name all the Cs.

How many Cs are on this keyboard? __5__

Trace these treble clefs.
Then write 3 treble clefs on your own.

Color the G line green.

Next, fill in the blanks.

__bass__ __clef__ ← Treble clef or bass clef?

__treble__ __clef__ ← Treble clef or bass clef?

F   C   G

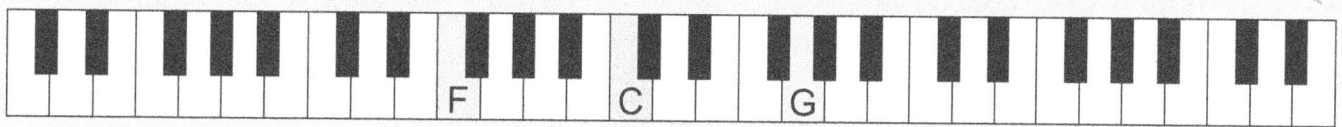

Name the colored keys.

Middle C on the Grand Staff

A __treble__ clef and a staff together make a treble *staff*.

I'm in the treble staff.

Trace the brace and line.

G line

Trace. Middle C

F line

I'm in the bass staff.

The grand staff

A __bass__ clef and a staff together make a bass *staff*.

The grand staff is for low notes *and* high notes.

Name the colored keys.

F   C   G

__bass__ __staff__ ← Treble staff or bass staff?   __treble__ __staff__ ← Treble staff or bass staff?

The grand staff is for __low__ notes *and* __high__ notes.

Let's write middle C.

Middle C

Here is a middle C. Trace it.
The line is called a *ledger line*.

Trace these too.

Trace them.

Circle the correct words:

The C near the middle of the piano is called   Little C   Fiddle C   ⟨Middle C⟩

Middle C has a line through it called a   ⟨ledger line⟩   edger line   hedger line

Below middle C we can find   higher sounds   ⟨lower sounds⟩   animal sounds

Above middle C we can find   ⟨higher sounds⟩   lower sounds   airplane noises

Doctor Mozart Music Theory Workbook, Answers for Level 1 & OB.   © MMVI, MMXVII Machiko and Paul Christopher Musgrave.   Published by April Avenue Music.   www.DoctorMozart.com

Be a Grand Staff Expert

Trace everything printed in gray.
Color the F line and G line.

Draw a grand staff and
middle C by yourself.

1
A

Green for
the G line.

Brace →

Yellow for
the F line.

Trace the brace and line.

A treble staff and bass staff
together make a __grand__ staff.

Fill in the blanks.

Middle C is
between
the staffs.

__bass__ __staff__ ← Treble staff
or bass staff?

__treble__ __staff__ ← Treble staff
or bass staff?

F   C   G

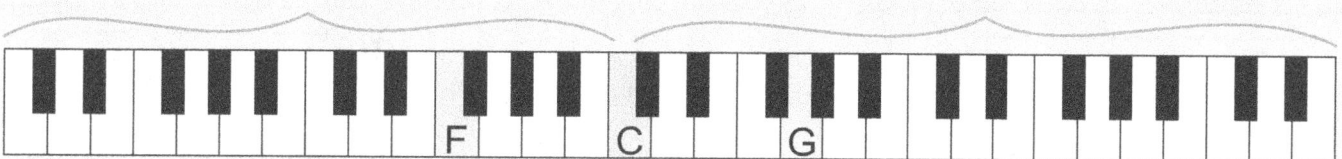

Name the colored keys.

Complete these grand staffs. Write a middle C on each.

Middle C has 2 Neighbors.

Bubble. Drip.

The lower neighbor is **B**. It looks like a floating **B**ubble.

B C D

The higher neighbor is **D**. It looks like a **D**rip waiting to fall.

D hangs below the treble staff, like a ___drip___ waiting to fall.
B is on top of the bass staff, like a ___bubble___ floating on water.

Trace. Draw lines to the keyboard.

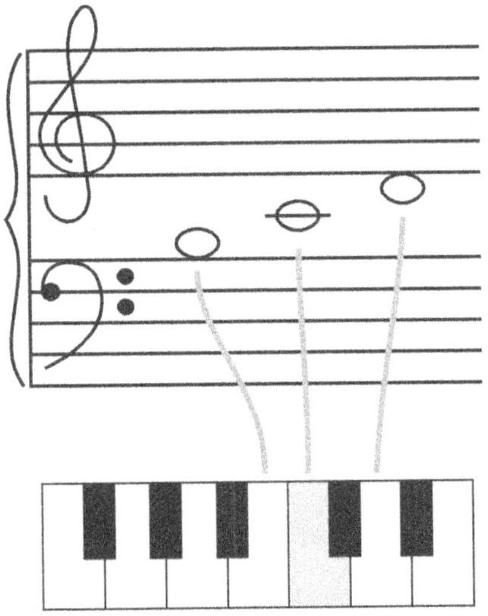

D for **D**rip

B for **B**ubble

Middle C is singing in the shower.

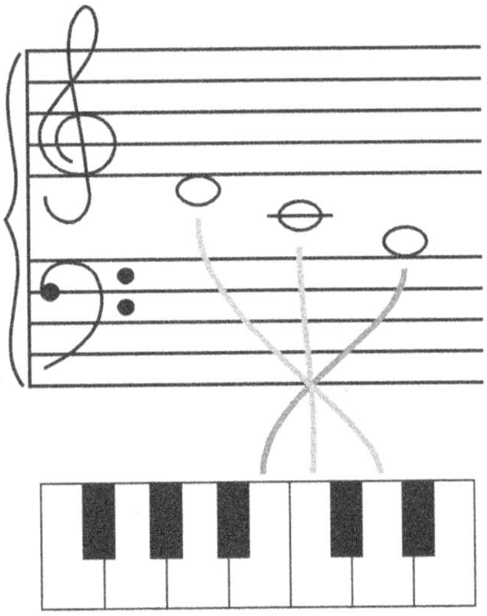

Trace the clefs. Write the notes.

Trace the notes. Circle the correct words and arrows.

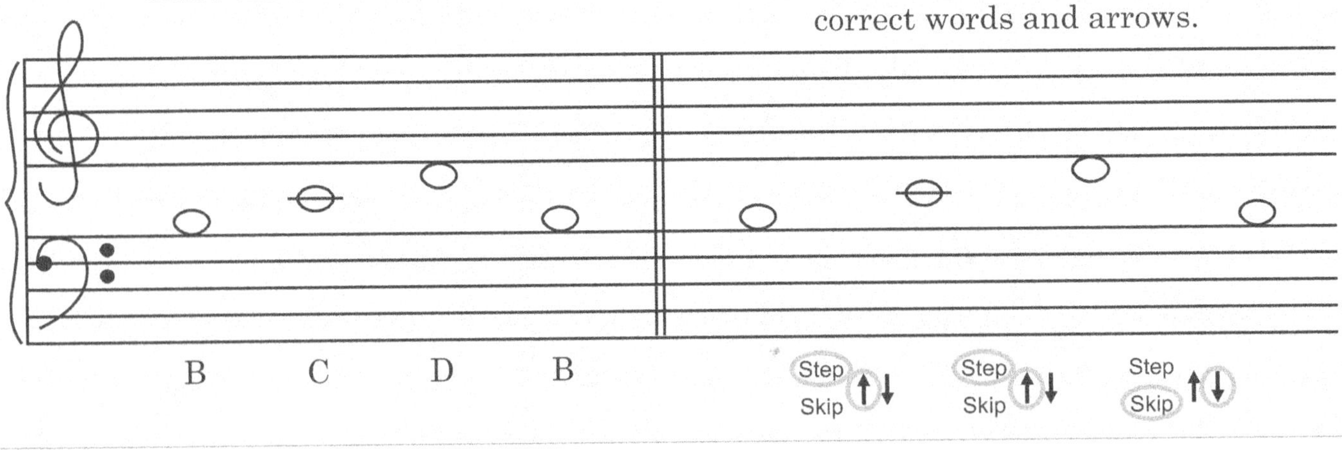

B   C   D   B

Step Skip ↑↓   Step Skip ↑↓   Step Skip ↑↓

Bubble and Drip Quiz

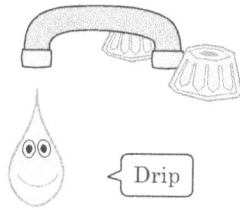

Drip

Name these notes.

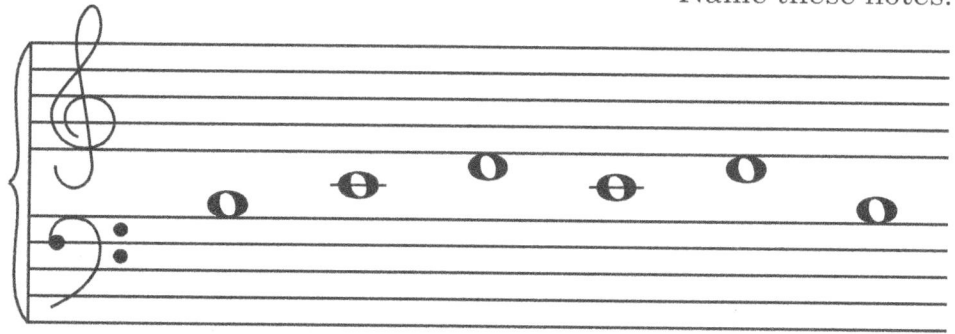

Trace.

1
A

B   C   D   C   D   B

Write middle C and its 2 neighbors.

Trace.

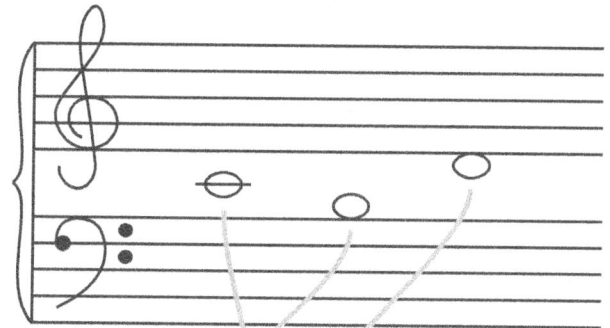

Draw lines to the keyboard.

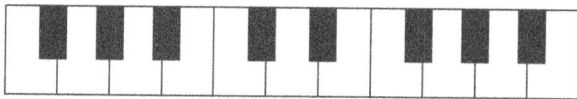

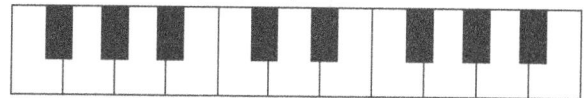

Bubble

Always start each staff with a clef. If a gray clef is already printed, trace it.

Next, color the F line and G line. Write the notes.

D hangs below the treble staff,
like a ___drip___ waiting to fall.
B is on top of the bass staff,
like a ___bubble___ floating on water.
The word *Drip* starts with a _d_.
The word *Bubble* starts with a _b_.

Trace.   B   C   D   B   D

The F Clef and G Clef

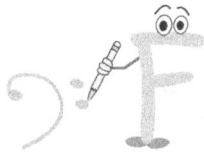

Why is the bass clef also called the F clef?

The bass clef has dots above and below the F line.

And it looks like a letter F.

It reminds us where F is.

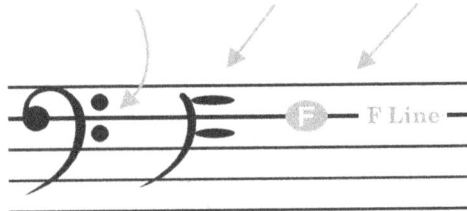

F Line

The bass clef has dots above and below the __F__ line

What is another name for the bass clef?
___F clef.___ What alphabet letter does the bass clef look like? __F__
Name the fourth line in the bass staff: __F__

Why is the treble clef also called the G clef?

The treble clef curls around the G line.

It looks like a letter G,

and it reminds us where G is.

G Line

The treble clef curls around the __G__ line

What is another name for the treble clef?
___G clef.___ What alphabet letter does the treble clef look like? __G__
Name the second line in the treble staff: __G__

Trace these notes. Name them.

Trace the lines. →

Name the notes.

F   B C D   G

All the Notes Between
F and G

Trace and name.

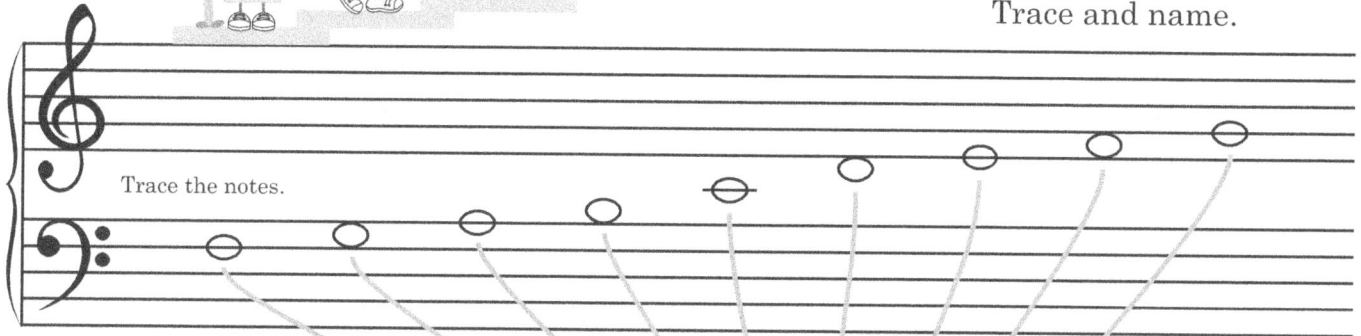

Trace the notes.

Trace the lines.

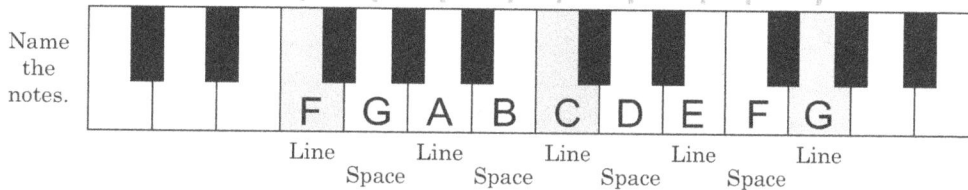

Name the notes.

F G A B C D E F G

Line   Line   Line   Line   Line
  Space   Space   Space   Space

Trace and name.

Draw lines.

F G A B C D E F G

If you step up from any space note, you will come to a __line__ note.

If you step up from any line note, you will come to a __space__ note.

Doctor Mozart Music Theory Workbook, Answers for Level 1 & OB.   © MMVI, MMXVII Machiko and Paul Christopher Musgrave.   Published by April Avenue Music.   www.DoctorMozart.com

F to G Challenge

Write the missing notes.

Trace the notes.

Draw lines.

Name the notes.

F	G	A	B	C	D	E	F	G

Line · Line · Line

Write all of the notes from F to G.

Draw lines.

Name the notes.

F	G	A	B	C	D	E	F	G

Circle the correct words and arrows.

Name the notes too.

Step

F   A   G

G   E   F

Skip

Step / Skip ↑↓   Step / Skip ↑↓

Step / Skip ↑↓   Step / Skip ↑↓

Measures and Bar Lines

Trace the bar lines.

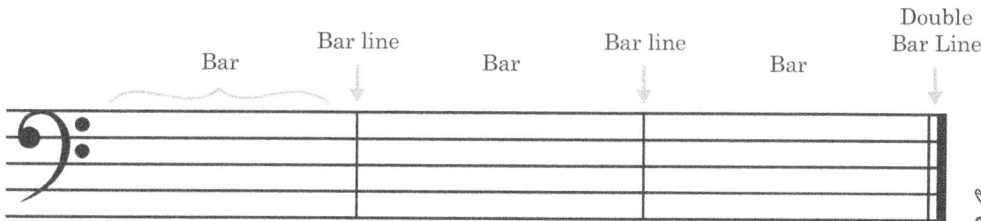

A double bar line is written at the very end of the music.

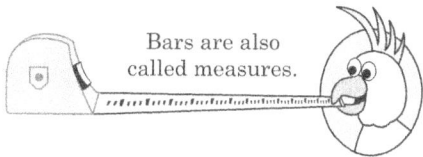

Bar   Bar line   Bar   Bar line   Bar   Double Bar Line

Bars are also called measures.

The area between two bar lines is called a ___**bar**___. Bars are separated from each other by ___**bar**___ lines. Bars are also called *measures*. Another word for *bar* is ___**measure**___.

This is a repeat sign. It has two lines and two dots.

Repeat Sign

At the very end of the music, we write a ___**double**___ bar line. A ___**repeat**___ sign tells you to repeat the music.

Another word for *measure* is ___**bar**___.

Draw lines to match the words with the signs.

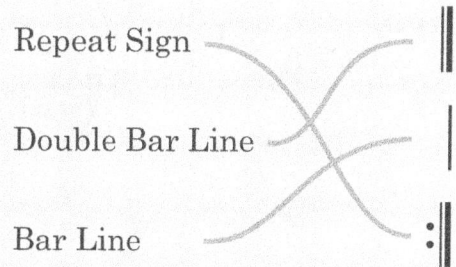

Repeat Sign

Double Bar Line

Bar Line

Trace everything printed in gray. Write the word **bar** above each measure.

Bars are like fields. And bar *lines* are like fences.

bar   bar   bar

Quarter, Half, and Whole Notes

Trace these notes.
Start with the head.
Then draw the stem.

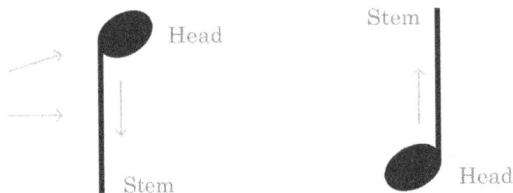

The round part is
called the ___head___.
The straight part is
called the ___stem___.

Quarter notes go at a medium walking speed. They get just **one beat** each.
What kind of note do you see at left? A ___quarter___ note.

How many beats does
each quarter note
usually get? _1_
Quarter notes are like
the steps you take
when you ___walk___.

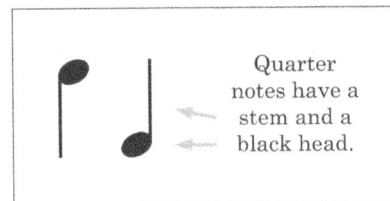

Trace.

Quarter
notes have a
stem and a
black head.

Half notes go slower, like slow skating.
The note at left is a ___half___ note.

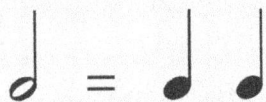

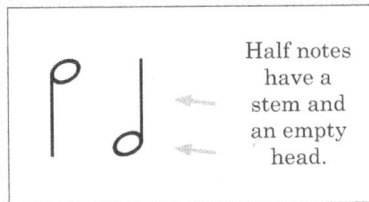

Trace.

Half notes
have a
stem and
an empty
head.

A half note is as long as 2 quarter notes.
A half note is as long as _2_ quarter notes.
Half notes go slowly, like slow ___skating___.

One **whole note** is as long as two half notes.

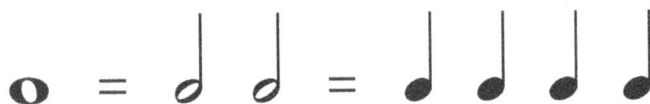

Trace.   Whole notes
have an
empty head
and no stem.

1 whole note is as long as _2_ half notes, or _4_ quarter notes.

4 ___quarter___ notes are as long as 2 ___half___ notes,
or 1 ___whole___ note.

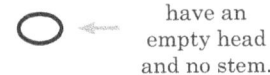

Doctor Mozart Music Theory Workbook, Answers for Level 1 & OB. © MMVI, MMXVII Machiko and Paul Christopher Musgrave.   Published by April Avenue Music.   www.DoctorMozart.com

CHOCOLatE Time

If two people share a chocolate bar, then each person can get half. If two people share, how much can each person get?

__Half__

In music, longer notes don't get more chocolate. Instead, they get more **time**. Long notes get more

_____time_____ .

How Friends Share Chocolate

If your friends don't want any, you can keep the **whole** chocolate bar. This whole chocolate bar has 4 pieces.

If your friends don't want any, you can have the
__whole__ chocolate bar.

How Notes Share Time

Whole notes don't share. One **whole note** gets **4 beats**, which is enough to fill a whole bar.

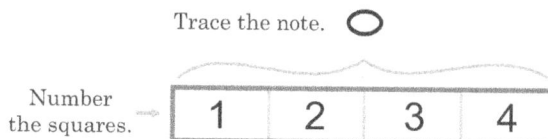

Trace the note. ⬭

Number the squares. →

| 1 | 2 | 3 | 4 |

Each whole note gets __4__ beats.

If two people share, then each person gets **half** of the bar.

If two people share, each person gets _____half_____ (2 pieces each).

These **half notes** get **2 beats** each.

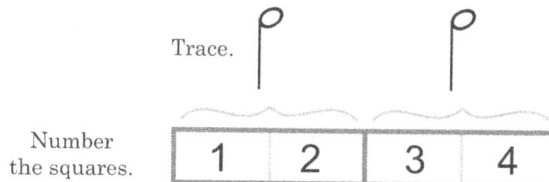

Trace.

Number the squares.

| 1 | 2 | 3 | 4 |

Half notes get __2__ beats each.
How many half notes can fit in this bar? __2__

If four people share, then each person gets **one quarter**.

If four people share, each person gets _____one quarter_____ (1 piece).

Quarter notes get only **1 beat** each.

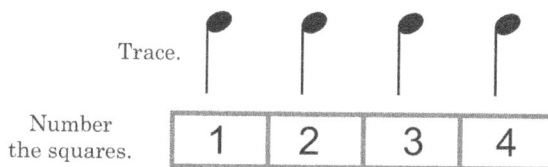

Trace.

Number the squares.

| 1 | 2 | 3 | 4 |

Quarter notes get __1__ beat each.
How many of them can fit in this bar? __4__

Doctor Mozart Music Theory Workbook, Answers for Level 1 & OB. © MMVI, MMXVII Machiko and Paul Christopher Musgrave.   Published by April Avenue Music.   www.DoctorMozart.com

Stem Up or Stem Down?

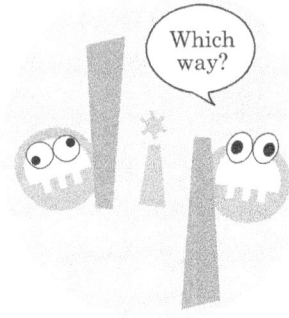

Which way?

These notes are **below** the middle line, so the stem goes **up**.

These notes are **on** the middle line, so the stem can go **up or down**.

These notes are **above** the middle line, so the stems go **down**.

—— Middle Line ——

Trace the notes

Each of these notes look like a letter **d**.

Each of these notes look like a letter **p**.

A note should look like a letter **d** or **p**. Remember the word **dip**. A note should *never* look like a letter b or q.

Which way should the stem go if the note is
below the middle line? ____Up.____
on the middle line? ____Up or down.____
above the middle line? ____Down.____

Circle the alphabet letters that notes can look like:

ⓓ ⓟ b q

What word can help you remember this? __Dip.__

Draw a stem on each note.

This stem can also go up.

Trace these notes.

Quarter note
Stem. ➡
Filled-in head. ➡

Half note
⬅ Stem.
⬅ Empty head.

Whole note
⬅ *No stem.*
⬅ Empty head.

How many quarter notes are these notes equal to?

𝅝 = 4   𝅗𝅥 = 2

How many quarter notes?

𝅗𝅥 + 𝅗𝅥 = 4

𝅘𝅥 + 𝅘𝅥 = 3

Doctor Mozart Music Theory Workbook, Answers for Level 1 & OB.   © MMVI, MMXVII Machiko and Paul Christopher Musgrave.   Published by April Avenue Music.   www.DoctorMozart.com

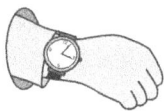

Time Signatures

These are time signatures. Trace them.
Then write them by yourself at the blue arrows.

Trace   Copy

Next, circle the top number of each time signature.

When the top number is 4, there are __4__ quarter notes in the bar.
When the top number is 3, there are __3__ quarter notes in the bar.

Circle the top number of each time signature.

How many
quarter notes
are in each bar?

4   3

Number the beats. Complete each time signature.

1   2   3   4   1   2   3   1   2   3   4

This is one of many possible answers.

Fill each bar with quarter notes. Number the beats.

1   2   3   1   2   3   4   1   2   3

Time Signature QUIZ

Number the beats. Complete each time signature.

1 2 3   1 2 3 4   1 2 3

1 whole note is as long as __2__ half notes, or __4__ quarter notes.

4 __quarter__ notes are as long as 2 __half__ notes, or 1 __whole__ note.

One, two, three, four.

Number the beats.

1 2 3 4 1 2 3 4 1 2 3 4

Each quarter note gets 1 beat.
Each half note gets 2 beats.

Tap while counting aloud.

1 2 3 4 1 2 3 4 1 2 3 4

Fill these bars with quarter notes and half notes. Number the beats.
This is one of many possible answers.

1 2 3 4 1 2 3 4 1 2 3 4

1 2 3 1 2 3 1 2 3 1 2 3

How many quarter notes are these notes as long as?

$o = 4$

$\downarrow = 2$

$\downarrow + \downarrow = 2$

$\downarrow + \downarrow = 4$

$\downarrow + \downarrow = 3$

How many quarter notes?

1
A

Draw a stem for each note.

What are the red arrows pointing at?

Bar Line   Double Bar Line   Repeat Sign

Number the beats. Complete each time signature.

Trace   1   2   3   4   1   2   3   1   2   3   4

Fill each bar with quarter notes and half notes.   *This is one of many possible answers.*

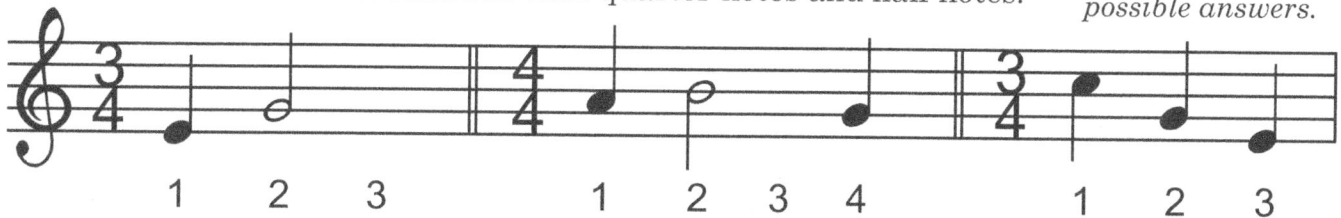

1   2   3   1   2   3   4   1   2   3

Doctor Mozart Music Theory Workbook, Answers for Level 1 & OB.   © MMVI, MMXVII Machiko and Paul Christopher Musgrave.   Published by April Avenue Music.   www.DoctorMozart.com

Meet the Space Note Cs

Trace and name.

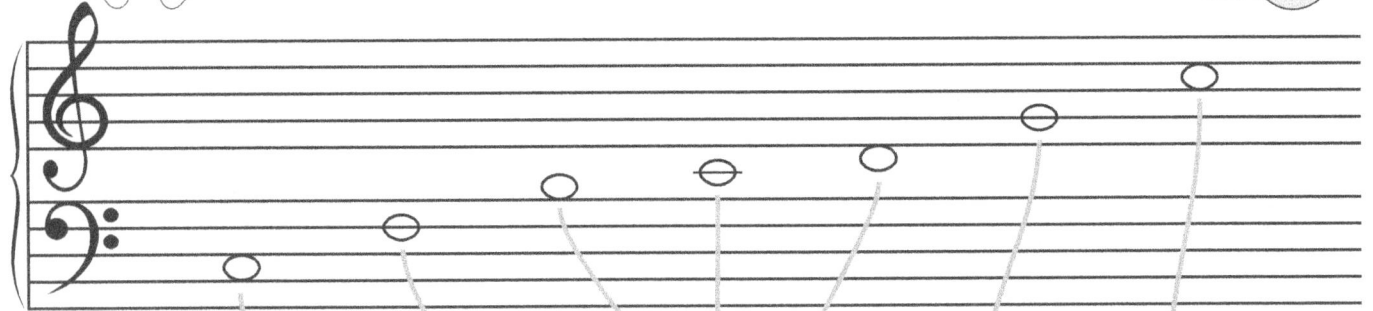

Draw lines.

C	F	B	C	D	G	C
Space	Line		Line		Line	Space

The low C is on the __2__ nd space   The high C is on the __3__ rd space.

Trace and name.

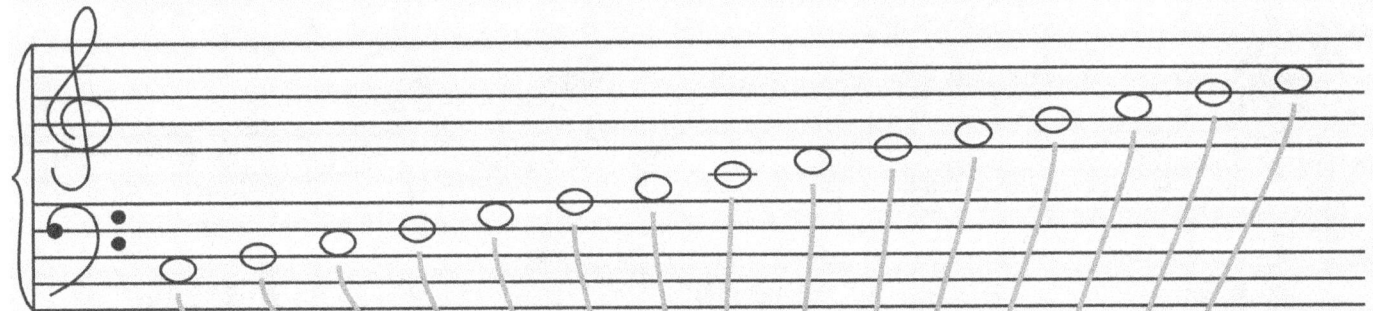

Draw lines.

C	D	E	F	G	A	B	C	D	E	F	G	A	B	C
Space							Line							Space

Write a note to match each alphabet character. Do not write middle C.

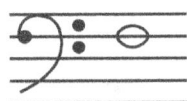

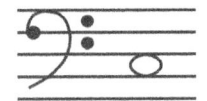

From C to C

Write all the notes between the two space note Cs.

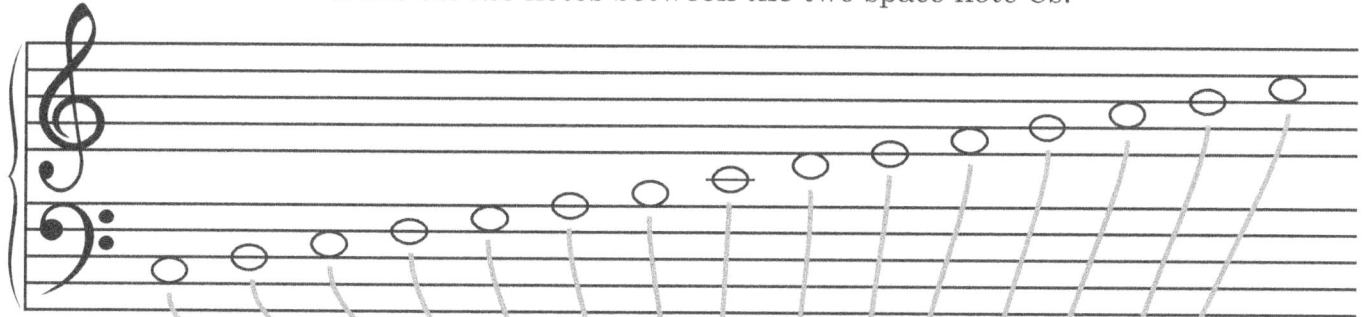

Draw lines.

Name the notes.

C D E F G A B C D E F G A B C

Next, for each colored key, write a note on the staff.

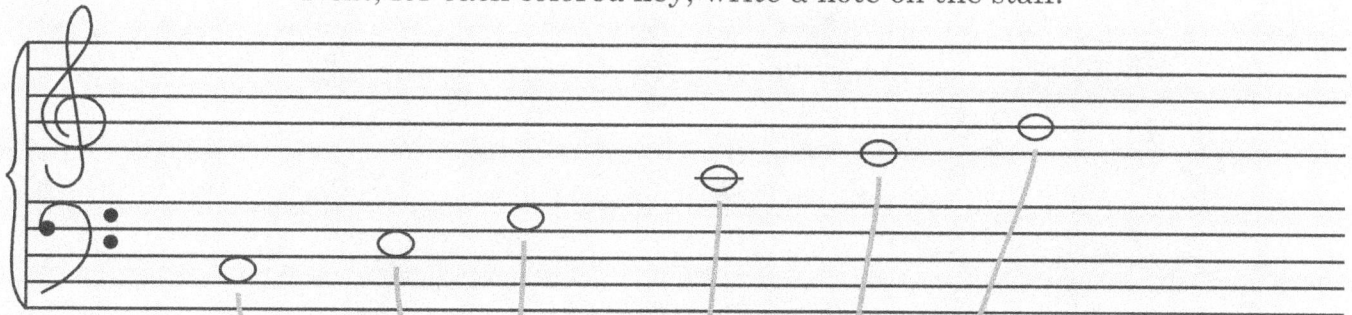

Draw lines.

Name the colored keys.

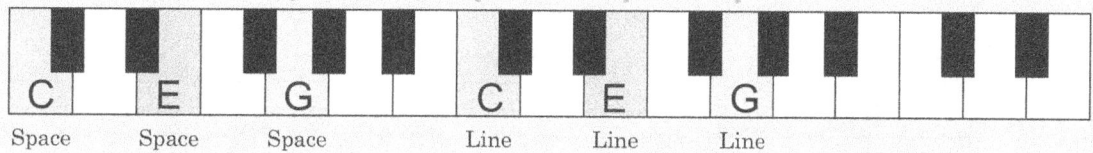

C E G C E G

Space Space Space Line Line Line

What 3 letter names do these colored keys have? C E G

These alphabet characters show the name of each note. Write the correct clef on each staff.

B   D   C   C   F   G

1
A

What is a Chord?

This is a chord. Say it like this: "kord".

A chord is a group of special notes played together. Here are two C chords.

Each C chord has 3 notes: C, E, & G.

Trace the notes.

Trace the lines.

Name the colored keys.

C E G C E G

Space Space Space Line Line Line

In each of these two chords, the lowest note is __C__.

A group of special notes played together is called a __chord__.

Write a C chord in each staff.

C chord →

C chord →

Draw lines.

Name the C chord notes.

C E G C E G

Space Line

C chord

The C chord has only *space* notes in the bass staff,
and only __line__ notes in the treble staff.

Doctor Mozart Music Theory Workbook, Answers for Level 1 & OB. © MMVI, MMXVII Machiko and Paul Christopher Musgrave. Published by April Avenue Music. www.DoctorMozart.com

Staff Test

Draw stems. Circle the correct words and arrows.

Write notes to match the words and arrows.

Write all the notes between the two space note Cs.

Draw lines.

Name the keys.

C D E F G A B C D E F G A B C

What is another name for the bass clef? **F clef.**

What is another name for the treble clef? **G clef.**

REVIEW QUIZ

Name these notes.

Draw lines.

C   F   B C D   G   C

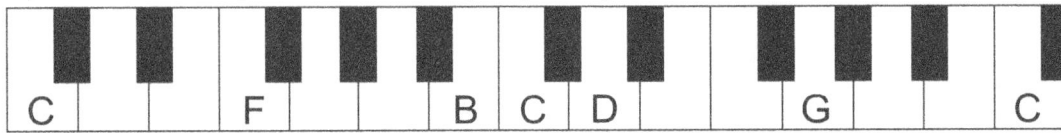

After each printed note, write a neighboring note. Follow the arrows.

Name the notes.

C D F G B C   D C G F C B

Step ↑   Step ↑   Step ↑   Step ↓   Step ↓   Step ↓

Next, write all the notes between the two space note Cs. Name the notes.

C D E F G A B C   C D E F G A B C

What are the red arrows pointing at?

Bar Line   Repeat Sign   Double Bar Line

Doctor Mozart Music Theory Workbook, Answers for Level 1 & OB. © MMVI, MMXVII Machiko and Paul Christopher Musgrave.   Published by April Avenue Music.   www.DoctorMozart.com

Tricky Quiz

Name the notes.

A E G F F G E A D B C C

Next, write the correct clef on each staff.

E   C   D   B

C   C   A   C

B   B   A   A

Write a C chord in each staff.

C chord →

C chord →

Draw lines.

Name the C chord notes.

C   E   G   C   E   G

1 A

Pro Quiz

Add the beats.

$$\text{♩(2)} + \text{♩(1)} = \boxed{3}$$ $$\quad \text{♩(1)} + \text{♩(1)} + \text{♩(1)} = \boxed{3}$$

$$\text{♩(2)} + \text{♩(2)} = \boxed{4}$$ $$\quad \text{♩(1)} + \text{♩(1)} + \text{♩(2)} = \boxed{4}$$

Number the beats. Complete each time signature.

1 2 3 4   1 2 3   1 2 3 4

Write an X under any bar that has too many or too few beats.

X   X   X

Complete each time signature. Fill the empty bars with notes. Number the beats.

This is one of many possible answers.

1 2 3 4   1 2 3 4   1 2 3   1 2 3

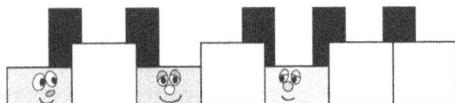

What 3 notes belong in a C chord? __C__ __E__ __G__
Below, circle the C chords.

Doctor Mozart® Music Theory Workbook Level 1B

In-Depth Piano Theory Fun for Children's Music Lessons and Home Schooling

Highly effective for beginners learning a musical instrument.

We will help you understand and remember each lesson.

1
B

Hi! I'm Doctor Mozart.

Doctor Mozart workbooks are filled with friendly cartoon characters. They make it fun to learn music theory in-depth. And in-depth music theory knowledge is essential for children learning a musical instrument. Use Doctor Mozart workbooks by themselves or with other teaching materials. Use them for music lessons and for home schooling.

The authors, Machiko and Paul Musgrave, are both graduates of Juilliard. Machiko has taught piano and theory at Soai University in Japan. Paul is an Associate of the Royal Conservatory of Music. The authors hope you enjoy using this book!

Many thanks to Kevin Musgrave for his meticulous proof-reading and insightful suggestions.
Created by Machiko and Paul Christopher Musgrave. Illustrated by Machiko Yamane Musgrave.   1.1.1

Doctor Mozart Music Theory Workbook, Answers for Level 1 & OB.   © MMVI, MMXVII Machiko and Paul Christopher Musgrave.   Published by April Avenue Music.   www.DoctorMozart.com

C to C Review

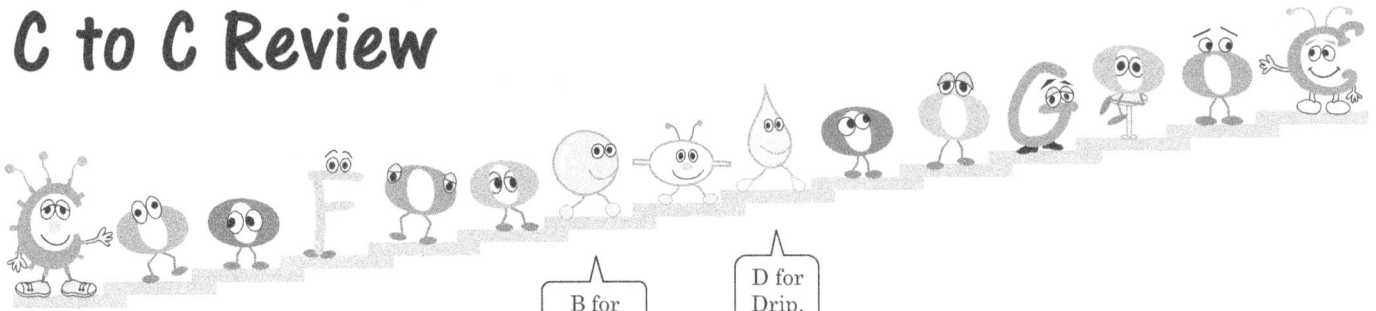

B for Bubble.

D for Drip.

Trace and name.

Trace the notes.

Draw lines.

Name the notes.

C D E F G A B C D E F G A B C

Space   Space

Write all the notes between the two space note Cs.

Draw lines.

Name the notes.

C D E F G A B C D E F G A B C

Space   Line   Space

Chord Review

Trace these C chords.

Trace the lines.

Name the chord notes.

C E G C E G

Space Space Space Line Line Line

1 B

Write a C chord in each staff.

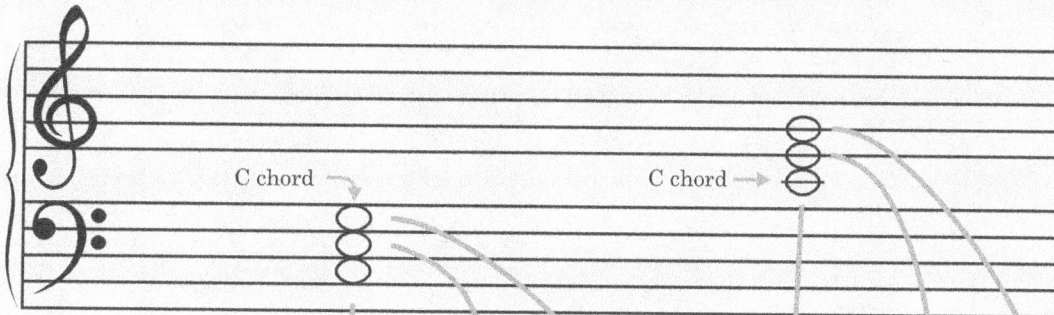

C chord

C chord →   C chord →

Draw lines.

Name the chord notes.

C E G C E G

The C chord has only *space* notes in the bass staff, and only <u>line</u> notes in the treble staff.

What 3 notes belong in a C chord? <u>C E G</u>
Circle the C chords.

Doctor Mozart Music Theory Workbook, Answers for Level 1 & OB. © MMVI, MMXVII Machiko and Paul Christopher Musgrave. Published by April Avenue Music. www.DoctorMozart.com

Treble Staff Elephants

Elephants Got Big Dirty Feet.

This elephant knows how to remember the treble staff line notes.

Feet — F
Dirty — D
Big — B
Got — G
Elephants — E

Trace the lines

Name the colored keys.

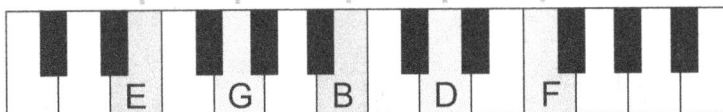

E G B D F

The sentence *Elephants Got Big Dirty Feet* helps us remember the treble staff __line__ notes.

Fill in the blanks: Elephants Got __big__ Dirty __feet__ .

Name these notes.

Draw lines.

C E G B D F

C E G B D F

Always start each staff with a clef. If a gray clef is already printed, trace it.

Write all the treble staff line notes.

Draw lines.

Name the notes.

E G B D F

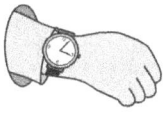

Time Signatures

Trace these time signatures. Then write them by yourself, at the arrows.

Trace   Copy

What do time signatures tell us?

3 3 beats per bar.

4 Each beat is as long as a quarter note.

This 3 on the top tells you that there are __3__ beats in each bar. You should count 1, 2, 3, 1, 2, 3.

This 4 on the bottom tells you that each beat is a ___quarter___ note in length.

Write an X under any bar that has too many or too few beats.

X   X

2 2 beats per bar.

2 Each beat is as long as a half note.

This 2 on the top tells you that there are __2__ beats in each bar. You should count 1, 2, 1, 2.

This 2 on the bottom tells you that each beat is a ___half___ note in length.

Number the beats. Complete the time signatures.

1   2   3   4   *   1   2   1   2   3

* Two bar lines come before a time signature change.

Doctor Mozart Music Theory Workbook, Answers for Level 1 & OB.   © MMVI, MMXVII Machiko and Paul Christopher Musgrave.   Published by April Avenue Music.   www.DoctorMozart.com

Elephant Checkup

What sentence can help you remember
the names of the treble staff line notes?

Elephants got big dirty feet.

Name these notes.

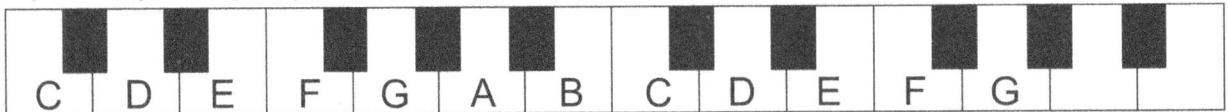

Draw lines.

E G B D F

C G B D F

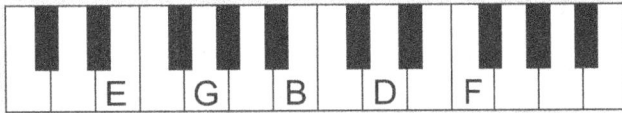

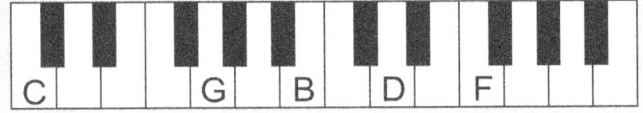

Write these treble staff notes.

Elephants   Big   Dirty   Got   Feet

After each line note, write a note that is one step higher.

One step higher.

Draw lines.

Name the notes.

C D E F G A B C D E F G

Doctor Mozart Music Theory Workbook, Answers for Level 1 & OB.   © MMVI, MMXVII Machiko and Paul Christopher Musgrave.   Published by April Avenue Music.   www.DoctorMozart.com

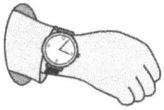

Time Signature Test

Write an X under any bar that has too many or too few beats.

X   X   X

Complete each time signature

Complete each time signature. Fill the empty bars with notes.

This is just one of many possible correct answers.

Number
the beats.   1 2 3 4   1 2 3 4   1 2 3   1 2 3

1 2   1 2   1 2   1 2   1 2   1 2

In a time signature, the __top__ number tells
you how many beats are in each bar.
The ___bottom___ number tells you whether
each beat is a quarter note or a half note, etc.

Fill each bar with any notes you like. Number the beats.   *This is one of many possible answers.*

1 2 3 4   1 2 3 4   1 2 3   1 2 3

Doctor Mozart Music Theory Workbook, Answers for Level 1 & 0B.   © MMVI, MMXVII Machiko and Paul Christopher Musgrave.   Published by April Avenue Music.   www.DoctorMozart.com

Great Big Dogs in the Bass Staff

This great big dog knows how to remember the bass staff line notes.

Great **Big** Dogs **Fight** Animals.

Animals —
Fight —
Dogs —
Big —
Great —

Trace.

Name the colored keys.
G B D F A

Complete the sentence: Great __Big__

Dogs __Fight__   __Animals__ .

This sentence can help you remember the bass staff __line__ notes.

Name these notes.

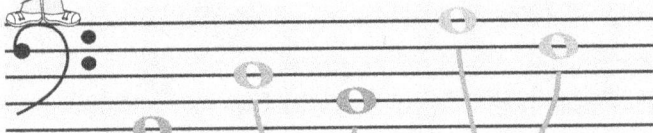

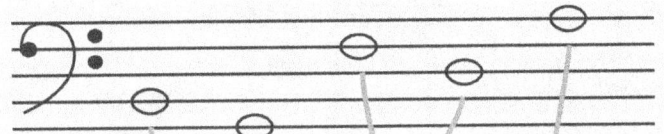

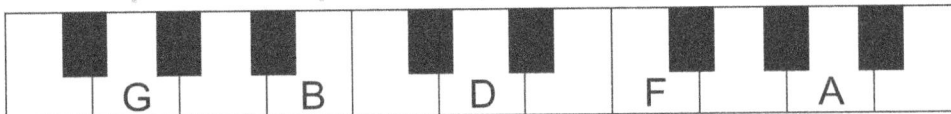

Draw lines.

Name the notes.
G B D F A

Trace.

G B D F A

Write all the bass staff line notes.

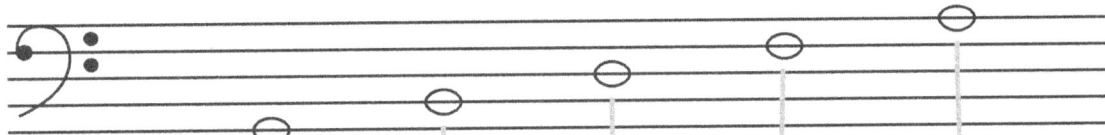

Draw lines.

Name the notes.
G B D F A

Doctor Mozart Music Theory Workbook, Answers for Level 1 & OB. © MMVI, MMXVII Machiko and Paul Christopher Musgrave. Published by April Avenue Music. www.DoctorMozart.com

B^Eat C^ount

Complete each time signature.
Fill the empty bars with notes.
Number the beats.

This is one of many possible answers.

1 2 3 4   1 2 3 4   1 2 3   1 2 3

Write an ampersand (&) under any notes that are between the beats.

1 2   1 2   1 & 2 &   1   2

Tap the half notes and quarter notes at the same time. Repeat until perfect.

Tap your **right hand** like the big feet stepping slowly.

Tap your **left hand** like the little feet, which step twice as fast.

Complete each time signature. Tap, hands together. Repeat until perfect.

What Do Cows Eat?

This cow knows how to remember the bass staff space notes.

All Cows Eat Grass.

G — Grass
E — Eat
C — Cows
A — All

Trace.

Name the colored keys.

A   C   E   G

Space   Space   Space   Space
    Line   Line   Line

Fill in the blanks:
All __Cows__ Eat __Grass__.

Space notes cannot be neighbors, because there are __line__ notes between them.

Name these bass staff notes.

Draw lines.

A   C   E   G

A   C   E   G

Write all the bass staff space notes.

Draw lines.

A   C   E   G

A   C   E   G

Name the notes.

Big Dog Exam

What sentence can help you remember
the names of the bass staff line notes?

Great Big Dogs Fight Animals.

Name these bass staff notes.

Draw lines.

G B D F A

G B D F A

Write these bass staff notes.

Great   Grass   Dogs   Fight   Cows   Animals   All   Big   Bubble

After each line note, write a note
that is one step higher.

One step higher.

Draw lines.

Name the notes.   G A B C D E F G A B

Doctor Mozart Music Theory Workbook, Answers for Level 1 & OB.   © MMVI, MMXVII Machiko and Paul Christopher Musgrave.   Published by April Avenue Music.   www.DoctorMozart.com

Bass Note Quiz

Name these bass staff notes.

Draw lines.

Name the notes.

G A B C D E F G A B

One step higher.

After each line note, write a note that is one step higher.

Draw lines.

Name the notes.

G A B C D E F G A B

Name these notes.

A G F E D C B A G

Write all the bass staff notes. Name them.

G A B C D E F G A B

Doctor Mozart Music Theory Workbook, Answers for Level 1 & OB. © MMVI, MMXVII Machiko and Paul Christopher Musgrave.   Published by April Avenue Music.   www.DoctorMozart.com

Review

Write a single note
in each blank.

Add the beats.

♩ + _♩_ = ♩

♩ + _♩_ + ♩ = o

♩ + _♩_ + ♩ = o

♩ + _♩_ + ♩ = o

Tap each rhythm, hands together. Repeat until perfect.

This is one of many possible answers.

Write your
own rhythm.
Tap it too!

Tap your rhythm. Practice until perfect.

This is one of many possible answers.

Make your own rhythm!

Doctor Mozart Music Theory Workbook, Answers for Level 1 & OB.   © MMVI, MMXVII Machiko and Paul Christopher Musgrave.   Published by April Avenue Music.   www.DoctorMozart.com

Treble Staff Giraffe

There are 2 Gs in the treble staff. The high G is named after me.

G for **Giraffe**

Drip, face, and giraffe.

G Line

Trace.

Name the treble staff space notes.

D F A C E G

Line   Space

Name these treble staff notes.

Draw lines.

D F G   C E G

D F G A   E G

Name these treble staff notes.

C C D D E E F F G G

These alphabet characters show the name of each note. Write the correct clef on each staff.

A F B G C E

Drip FACE Giraffe Elephants

Here are all the treble staff notes you have learned.

Feet
Dirty
Big
Got
Elephants

E C A F

Draw lines.

Name the notes.

C D E F G A B C D E F G

Name these treble staff notes.

Draw lines.

Name the notes.

D E F G A B C D E F G

Name these treble staff notes.

G D E F F E B D G

Draw a treble clef. Write the notes.

Got   Big   Dirty   Elephants   Feet   Drip   Giraffe

Doctor Mozart Music Theory Workbook, Answers for Level 1 & OB. © MMVI, MMXVII Machiko and Paul Christopher Musgrave.   Published by April Avenue Music.   www.DoctorMozart.com

Mr. Bass Staff Foot

Foot, cows, bubble.

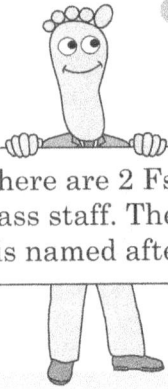

F Line

F for Foot

There are 2 Fs in the bass staff. The low F is named after me.

Trace

F A C E G B

Space   Name the space notes.   Line

Name these bass staff notes.

Draw lines.

F A E F G B

F C E F G B

Name these bass staff notes.

F F G G A A B B C

Write the correct clef on each staff.

Foot Cows Bubble Dogs

Here are all the bass staff notes you have learned.

Animals Fight Dogs Big Great

Grass Eat Cows All

Draw lines.

Name the notes.

F G A B C D E F G A B

A B C D E F G

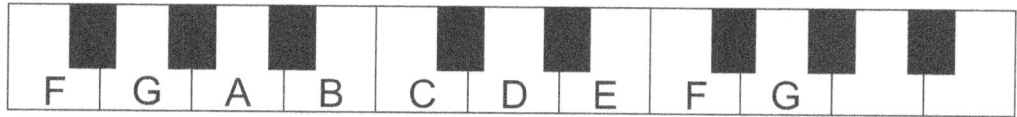

Name these bass staff notes.

Draw lines.

F G A B C D E F G

Name these bass staff notes.

B   F   G   A   A   G   D   F   B

Write these bass staff notes.

Grass   Great   Dogs   Fight   Foot   Cows   All   Animals   Big   Bubble

Doctor Mozart Music Theory Workbook, Answers for Level 1 & OB.   © MMVI, MMXVII Machiko and Paul Christopher Musgrave.   Published by April Avenue Music.   www.DoctorMozart.com

1 B

Quarter Rests

When you talk, you hear your voice. But as you take a breath, your voice is silent. Music has silences too. We write them with special signs called **rests**.

These are the same length.

quarter rest   quarter note

A silence in music is called a __rest__.

A quarter rest is as long as a __quarter__ note.

Next, answer with a single note that has the same time value.

𝄽 = ♩   𝄽 + 𝄽 = 𝅗𝅥   𝄽 + 𝄽 + 𝄽 + 𝄽 = 𝅝

A quarter rest looks like a zig-zag above a curl. Trace these quarter rests. Then write 3 more.

You can start from the top or the bottom.

Curl around the 2nd line.

Number the beats. Write quarter rests for any missing beats.

| 1 | 2 | 3 | 4 | | 1 | 2 | 3 | 4 | | 1 | 2 | 3 | | 1 | 2 | 3 |

Add the quarter note beats.

♩ + 𝄽 = ☐ 2
1   1

𝅗𝅥 + 𝄽 + ♩ = ☐ 4
2   1   1

𝅝 − 𝄽 = ☐ 3
4   1

𝅗𝅥 − 𝄽 = ☐ 1
2   1

TREBLE TEST

Name these treble staff notes.

F   E   A   G   C   B   E   D   G   F

C   C   D   D   E   E   F   F   G   G

Draw a treble clef. Write two notes for each letter, as shown above.

C   C   D   D   E   E   F   F   G   G

Write 8 different treble staff notes. Name them.

This is one of many possible answers.

Draw lines.

D   F G   B C   E F G

Half Rests   # Whole Rests

Same length.   Same length.

A half rest looks like a hat.

Trace and draw 3 more.   3rd space   Trace and draw 3 more.

Whole rests and half rests are both written in the __3__ rd space. Write the rests shown.

4
3
2
1

half   whole   quarter   half   quarter   whole

Write rests that have the number of beats shown.

Example

1   2

4
3
2
1

2   1   4   1   2   4

A whole rest looks like a hole in the ground.

In each box, write the total number of quarter note beats.

Two quarter rests equal one half rest.

𝄽 + ▬ + 𝅝 = 7

▬ – 𝄽 = 1

𝅝 + ▬ + ♩ = 9

▬ + 𝄽 + 𝄽 = 4

▬ – ▬ = 2

BASS TEST

Name these bass staff notes.

G F B A D C F E A G

F F G G A A B B C C

1
B

Draw a bass clef. Write two notes for each letter, as shown above.

F F G G A A B B C C

This is just one of many possible correct answers.

Write 8 different bass staff notes. Name them.

Draw
lines.

Bass Trio

F A B D E F G B Middle

Doctor Mozart Music Theory Workbook, Answers for Level 1 & OB. © MMVI, MMXVII Machiko and Paul Christopher Musgrave.   Published by April Avenue Music.   www.DoctorMozart.com

REVIEW QUIZ

Write a single rest to complete each bar. Number the beats. Tap the rhythms.

In each box, write the total number of quarter note beats.

Write a treble clef and a 4 / 4 time signature.
Fill the bars with notes.

Number
the beats.
This is just one of many possible correct answers.

Include some quarter rests and half rests.

Write a bass clef and a 3 / 4 time signature. Fill the bars with notes.

Number
the beats.
This is just one of many possible correct answers.

Doctor Mozart Music Theory Workbook, Answers for Level 1 & OB. © MMVI, MMXVII Machiko and Paul Christopher Musgrave.   Published by April Avenue Music.   www.DoctorMozart.com

TREBLE EXAM

Write these treble staff notes.

Remember the clefs.

| Elephant | Big | Feet | Giraffe | Dirty | Drip | Got |

After each printed note, write a note that is one step lower.

<u>G</u> <u>F</u> <u>E</u> <u>D</u> <u>C</u> <u>B</u> <u>A</u> <u>G</u> <u>F</u> <u>E</u>

Name the notes.

1
B

Name these treble staff notes.

B A C G D F E E F

C C D D E E F F G G

Write all the treble staff notes, stepping down. Name them.

G F E D C B A G F E D C

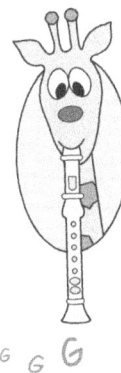

Doctor Mozart Music Theory Workbook, Answers for Level 1 & OB. © MMVI, MMXVII Machiko and Paul Christopher Musgrave. Published by April Avenue Music. www.DoctorMozart.com

Time Signature Exercise

26

Number the beats. Draw the missing bar lines.

1 2 3 4   1 2 3 4   1 2 3 4   1 2 3 4

1 2 3   1 2 3   1 2 3   1 2 3   1 2 3   1 2 3

1 2 3 4   1 2 3 4   1 2 3 4   1 2 3 4   1 2 3 4

Number the beats. Complete each time signature.

Write an ampersand (&) under any notes that are between the beats.

1 2 3 4   1 2 3 4   1   2 &   1 & 2 &

Tap while counting aloud.

Write a clef and a time signature. Fill some bars with notes and rests.

Write your own music.

1 2 3 4   1 2 3 4   1 2 3 4

Number the beats.

This is just one of many possible correct answers.

Doctor Mozart Music Theory Workbook, Answers for Level 1 & OB.   © MMVI, MMXVII Machiko and Paul Christopher Musgrave.   Published by April Avenue Music.   www.DoctorMozart.com

BASS EXAM

Write these bass staff notes.

Remember the clefs.

Foot   Dogs   Big   Bubble   Animals   Grass   Cows

Name these bass staff notes.

D   C   E   B   F   A   G   G   A

After each printed note, write a note that is one step lower.

B A   A G   G F   F E   E D   D C   C B   B A   A G

Name the notes.

Name these bass staff notes.

E   F   F   G   G   A   A   B   B   C

Write all the bass staff notes, stepping down. Name them.

C B A G F E D C B A G F

Accent Your Music

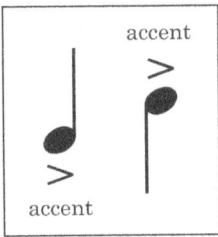

Trace the accents at left (>). If a note has an accent mark, you should play it louder.

Accented notes should be played __louder__.

Next, draw note stems and bar lines.
Write an accent on the first note of each bar.

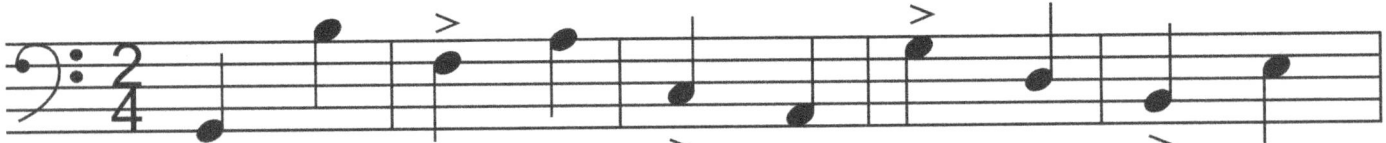

Name the notes. G B F A C A G D B E

Crescendo and Diminuendo

Crescendo means gradually get louder. *Diminuendo* means gradually get softer.
Here are the musical signs:

Kre-SHEN-doe

Dim-in-u-EN-do

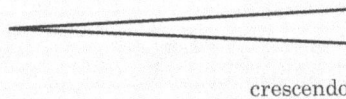
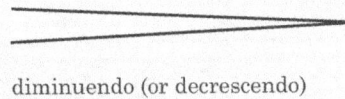

crescendo

diminuendo (or decrescendo)

__crescendo__ means gradually get louder. __diminuendo__ means gradually get softer.

Draw lines to match each term with its meaning.

crescendo (cresc.) —————— Play gradually more softly.

decrescendo (or decresc.) —————— Play gradually louder.

diminuendo (or dim.) —————— Play the note louder.

accent ——————

Number the beats. Draw bar lines. Write some cresc. and dim. signs.

Trace.

(Example answer)

1 2 3 4   1 2 3 4   1 2 3 4   1 2 3 4

Treble & Bass Quiz

Name these treble staff notes.

C C D D E E F F G G

Draw a treble clef. Write two notes for each letter, as shown above.

C C D D E E F F G G

1 B

What are the red arrows pointing at?

bar line   double bar line   repeat sign

Name these bass staff notes.

F F G G A A B B C C

Draw a bass clef.
Write two notes for each letter, as shown above.

F F G G A A B B C C

The Grand Staff Meets the Keyboard

Name these notes.

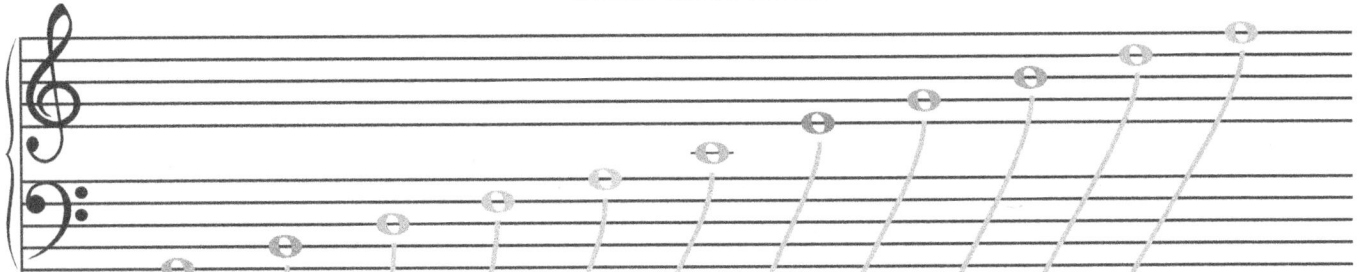

Draw lines.

G B D F A C E G B D F

Draw lines.

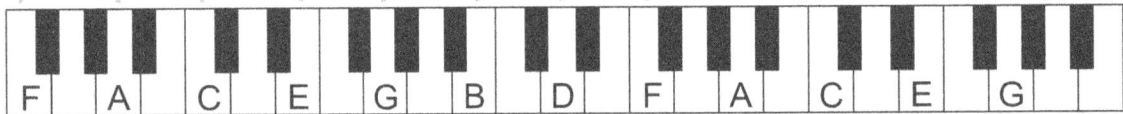

F A C E G B D F A C E G

Write each paw print note on this grand staff.

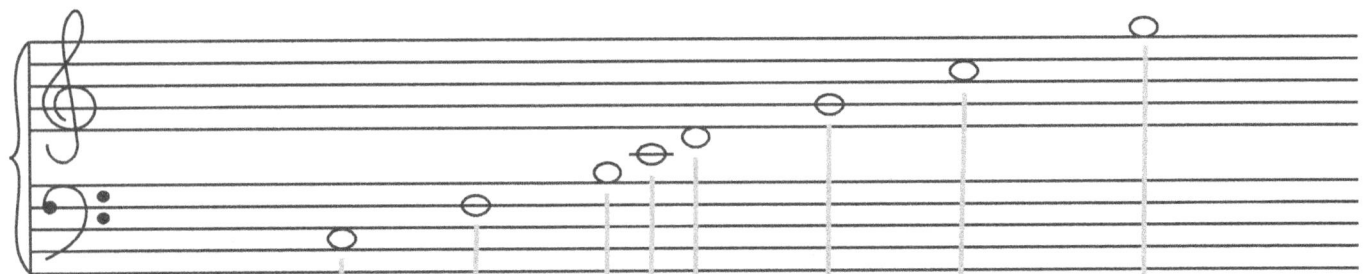

Draw lines.

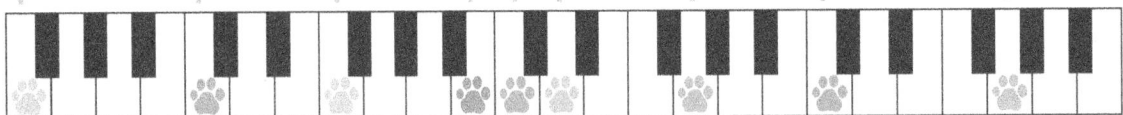

Dynamics Marks

Fill in the blanks. Trace the arrows.

_pp_

_pp_ = pianissimo

Play or sing very softly.

Pianissimo = *pp*

_p_

_p_ = piano

Play or sing softly.

Piano = *p*

_mp_

_mp_ = mezzo piano

Medium quiet, a little louder than *piano.*

Mezzo piano = *mp*

_mf_

_mf_ = mezzo forte

Medium loud, a little louder than *mezzo piano.*

Mezzo forte = *mf*

_f_

_f_ = forte

Play or sing loudly.

Forte = *f*

Signs that tell you how soft or loud to play are called dynamics marks.

_ff_

_ff_ = fortissimo

Play or sing very loudly.

Fortissimo = *ff*

Number these dynamics marks, from 1 for the quietest, to 6 for the loudest.

p	*mp*	*mf*	*ff*	*pp*	*f*
2	3	4	6	1	5

Signs that tell you how soft or loud to play are called ____dynamics____ marks.

1
B

GRAND STAFF EXPERT QUIZ

Complete each grand staff. Name the notes.

F F F F G G G A A A B B B C C C D D D E E E

F D G E A F B G C A D B E C F D G E A F B G

D C C D B E A F G G F

D B E A F G G F A E B

Make a grand staff. Name the notes.

Draw lines.

F G B C D F B C D G B C D F G

Staccato

Staccato

Staccato

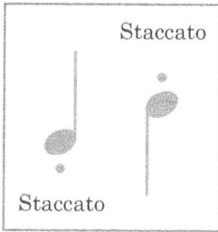

At left, the dots make the notes staccato. Let go of staccato notes immediately after you play them. If a note has a staccato mark, you should let go __immediately__.

Next, draw stems and bar lines. Then find an empty space near each note head, and write a dot in it.

Name the notes. F A B E G C A C

1 B

Legato

Trace the slurs.

slur

slur

Trace the slurs at left. A slur tells you to play **legato**, which means join the notes as you play them. Legato is the opposite of staccato.

The opposite of staccato is __legato__.

Marks that tell you whether to play staccato or legato are called **articulation marks**. Staccato and legato marks are called __articulation__ marks.

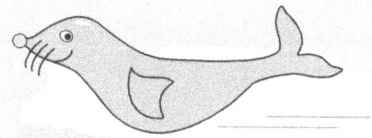

Fermata MOLTO Poco

The fermata sign tells you to pause on a note or a rest.

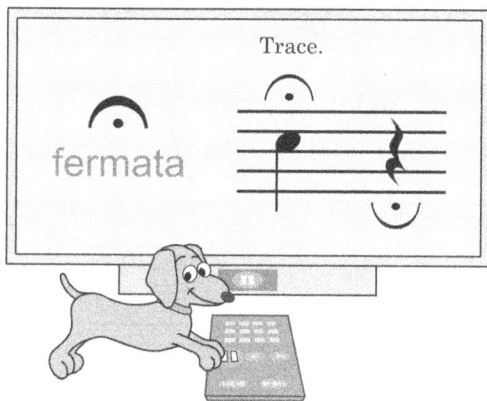

fermata

Trace.

Molto means very much.

Molto allegro means very fast.

Poco means a little.

Poco a poco means gradually.

Write the correct terms.   A little __poco__   Very much __molto__   Pause __fermata__

GRAND STAFF PRO EXAM

Draw the clefs. Name the notes.

F F F F G G G A A A B B B C C C D D D E E E

G F E D C B A G F E D

B A G F E D C B A G F

Write a different note for each letter.

F F F F F F G G G G A A A

Different notes.

B B B C C C D D D E E E

Doctor Mozart Music Theory Workbook, Answers for Level 1 & OB.   © MMVI, MMXVII Machiko and Paul Christopher Musgrave.   Published by April Avenue Music.   www.DoctorMozart.com

Notes & Clefs

Name the notes.

B F D G G A F E A G E F D B

F F F F G G G G A A A B B B C C C

Write the correct clef on each staff.

G E F A

G G E E

F D D F

Doctor Mozart Music Theory Workbook, Answers for Level 1 & OB. © MMVI, MMXVII Machiko and Paul Christopher Musgrave.   Published by April Avenue Music.   www.DoctorMozart.com

Dynamics & Articulation Quiz

Draw a line from each *sign* to its *name*, and then to its *meaning*.

ff Fortissimo Trio *ff*

Pianissimo
pp Recital *pp*

Sign	Name	Meaning
♩	piano	Play the note louder
>	accent	Soft
p	fortissimo	Very loud
ff	pianissimo	Very soft
▷ (decrescendo)	diminuendo (dim.) or decrescendo (decresc.)	Gradually get softer
pp	forte	Gradually get louder
◁ (crescendo)	crescendo (cresc.)	Loud
f	mezzo piano	A little louder than *p*
mf	mezzo forte	A little louder than *mp*
mp	fermata	Let go of the note immediately
(staccato dot)	staccato	Pause
(fermata)		

Next, name what each blue arrow is pointing to.

accent   staccato   slur   diminuendo   fermata

mp   crescendo   mf   bar line   pp   pianissimo   repeat sign

mezzo piano   crescendo   mezzo forte

NOTE TEST

Each pair of these notes should have the same name. Write the clefs. Name the notes.

G   G   A   A

G   G   C   C

E   E   F   F

Write some slurs, staccato marks, and fermata signs.

These are some examples of correct answers.

Next, write a time signature on each staff. Fill the bars with notes, rests, and musical signs. Number the beats.

1 2 3 1 2 3 1 2 3 1 2 3

mf   *mp*

1 2 3 4 1 2 3 4 1 2 3 4 1 2 3 4

Musical Review

Tap these rhythms. Repeat until perfect.

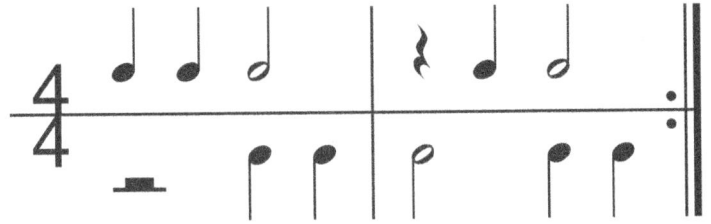

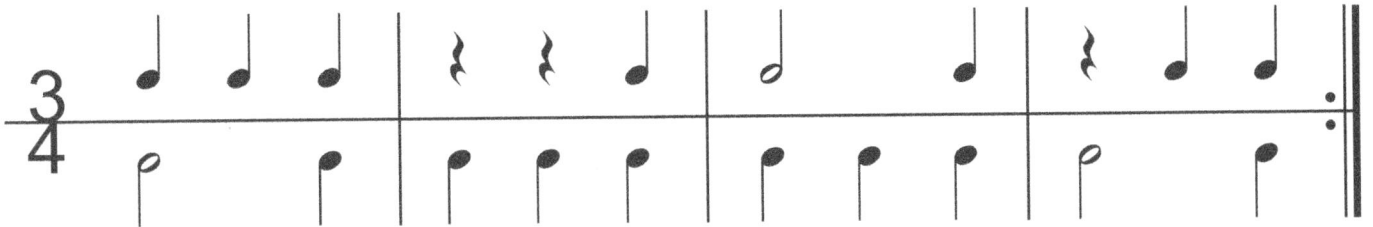

Draw lines to the right answers.

How to remember the bass staff line notes.

How to remember the bass staff space notes.

poco

molto

staccato

legato or slurred

D for drip

B for bubble

The treble staff space notes spell FACE.

How to remember the treble staff line notes.

decrescendo or diminuendo

fermata

Doctor Mozart® Music Theory Workbook

In-Depth Piano Theory Fun for Children's Music Lessons and Home Schooling

We will help you remember each lesson.

Learning theory will help you play music better.

Level 1C – Contents

1 C

Hi! I'm Doctor Mozart.

Highly effective for beginners learning a musical instrument.

Doctor Mozart workbooks are filled with friendly cartoon characters. They make it fun to learn music theory in-depth. And in-depth music theory knowledge is essential for children learning a musical instrument. Use Doctor Mozart workbooks by themselves or with other teaching materials. Use them for music lessons and for home schooling.

The authors, Machiko and Paul Musgrave, are both graduates of Juilliard. Machiko has taught piano and theory at Soai University in Japan. Paul is an Associate of the Royal Conservatory of Music. The authors hope you enjoy using this book!

Many thanks to Kevin Musgrave for his meticulous proof-reading and insightful suggestions.

Created by Machiko and Paul Christopher Musgrave. Illustrated by Machiko Yamane Musgrave.   1.1.0

Doctor Mozart Music Theory Workbook, Answers for Level 1 & OB.   © MMVI, MMXVII Machiko and Paul Christopher Musgrave.   Published by April Avenue Music.   www.DoctorMozart.com

Tempo Terms: How Fast to Play

Here are some special words that tell you how fast
to play or sing. Trace and write each tempo term.

Tempo is the
speed of music.

Tempo

Trace. **Prestissimo**
(as fast as possible)

Write. Prestissimo

Presto
(very fast)

Presto

Allegro
(fast)

Allegro

Allegretto
(a little slower than allegro)

Allegretto

Moderato
(at a medium tempo)

Moderato

Andantino
(a little faster than andante)

Andantino

Andante
(at a slow walking pace)

Andante

Adagio
(slower than andante)

Adagio

Larghetto
(a little faster than largo)

Larghetto

Largo or Lento
(very slow)

Largo

Lento

TEMPO TERMINOLOGY TEST

Write the tempo terms in order from slow to fast.

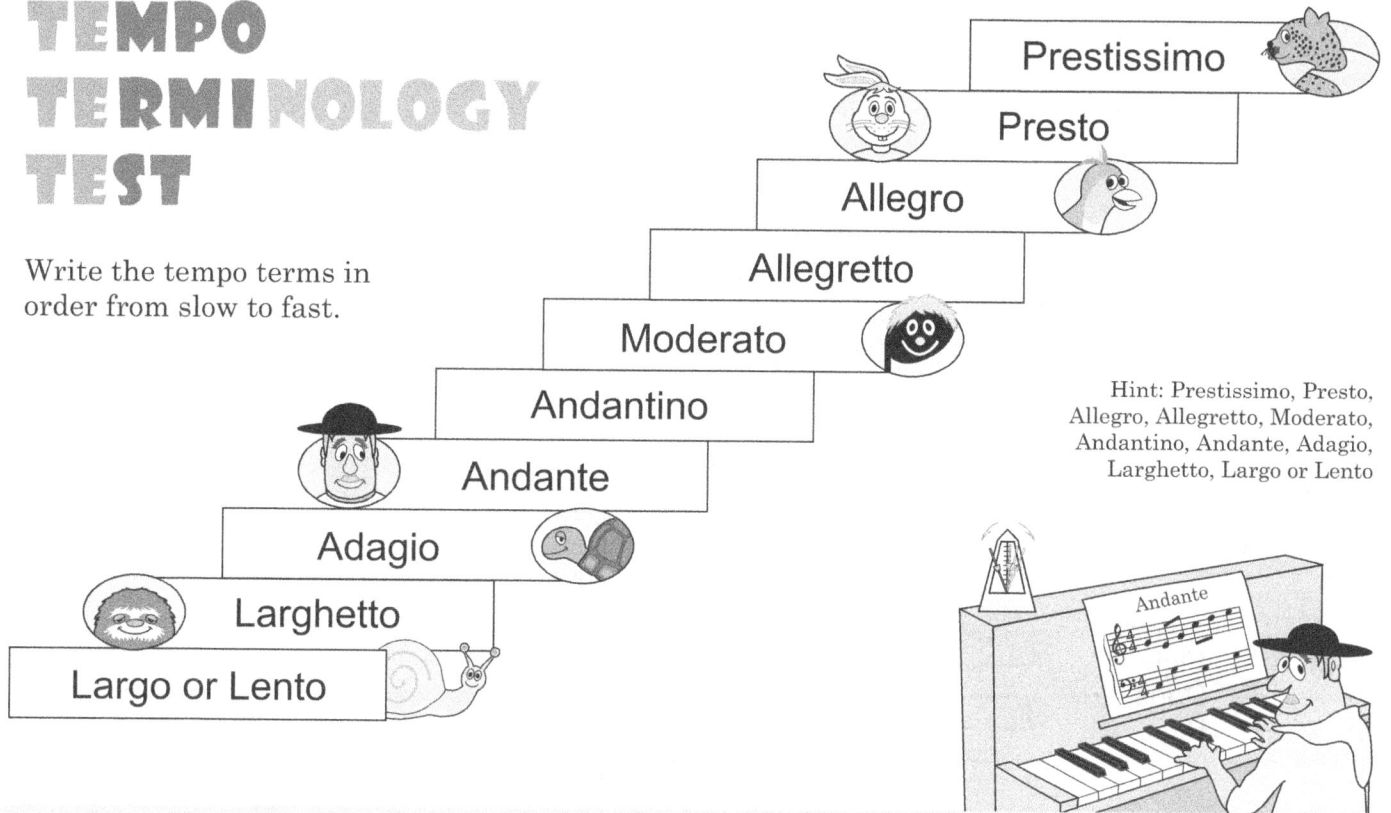

Prestissimo

Presto

Allegro

Allegretto

Moderato

Andantino

Andante

Adagio

Larghetto

Largo or Lento

Hint: Prestissimo, Presto, Allegro, Allegretto, Moderato, Andantino, Andante, Adagio, Larghetto, Largo or Lento

Andante

Write the correct terms. Draw lines to match the terms with their meanings.

Prestissimo   as fast as possible ___Prestissimo___

Presto   very fast ___Presto___

Allegro   fast ___Allegro___

Allegretto   a little slower than allegro ___Allegretto___

Moderato   at a medium tempo ___Moderato___

Andantino   a little faster than andante ___Andantino___

Andante   at a slow walking pace ___Andante___

Adagio   slower than andante ___Adagio___

Larghetto   A little faster than largo ___Larghetto___

Largo or Lento   very slow ___Largo or Lento___

1
C

Number the terms from slow to fast. Draw lines to the correct meanings.

__4__ Allegro   ● very fast

__5__ Presto   ● fast

__2__ Andante   ● at a moderate or medium tempo

__3__ Moderato   ● at a slow walking pace

__1__ Largo or Lento   ● very slow

Grand Staff Note Review

Write the words and sentences that match the grand staff note names.

Trace.

Feet
Dirty
Big
Got
Elephants

E
C
A
F

G for Giraffe

D for Drip

B for Bubble

Animals
Fight
Dogs
Big
Great

Grass
Eat
Cows
All

F for Foot

Hint: Elephants Got Big Dirty Feet. FACE. Great Big Dogs Fight Animals. All Cows Eat Grass. Foot, Bubble, Drip, Giraffe.

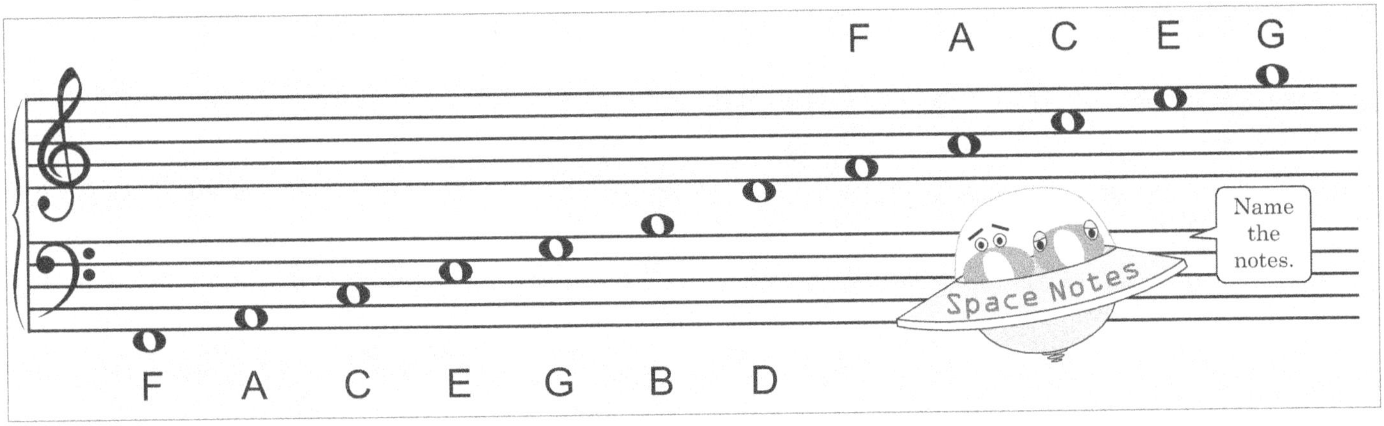

F A C E G

F A C E G B D

Name the notes.

Space Notes

Name these notes on the keyboard.

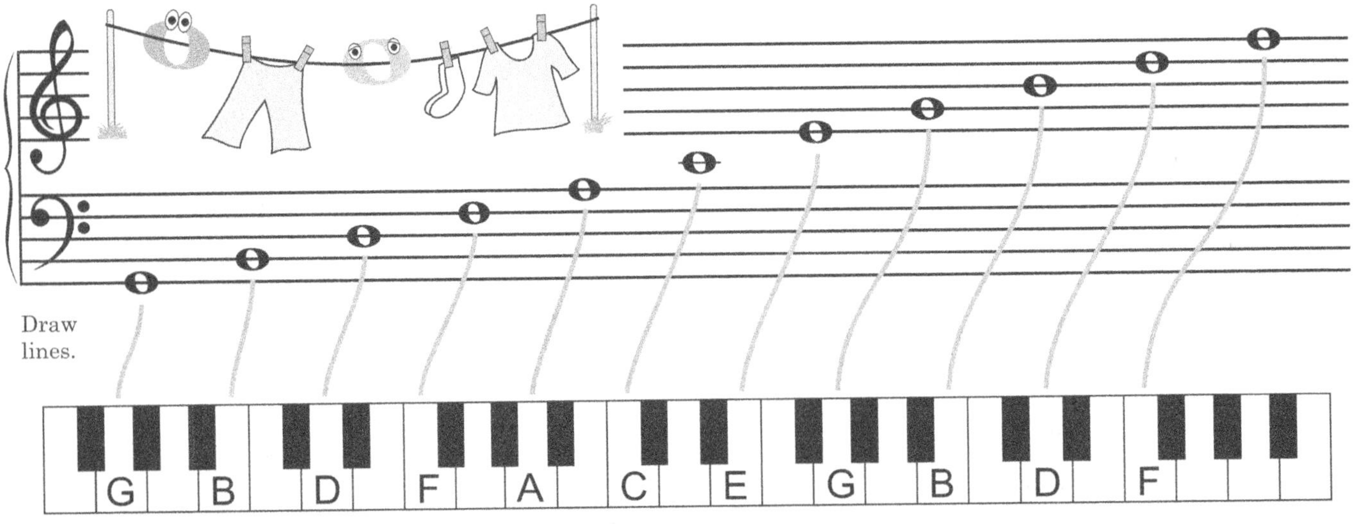

Draw lines.

G B D F A C E G B D F

Doctor Mozart Music Theory Workbook. Answers for Level 1 & OB. © MMVI, MMXVII Machiko and Paul Christopher Musgrave. Published by April Avenue Music. www.DoctorMozart.com

GRAND STAFF EXPERT
QUIZ

Draw the clefs. Name the notes.

D E F G A B C D E F G

B A G F E D C B A G F

F F F F G G G A A A B B B C C C D D D E E E

G B F A E G D F C E B D A C G B F A E G D F

Always draw the clefs first, even if I don't remind you.

Draw lines.

Name the notes.

F G | B C D | F | B C D | G | B C D | F G

Doctor Mozart Music Theory Workbook, Answers for Level 1 & OB.   © MMVI, MMXVII Machiko and Paul Christopher Musgrave.   Published by April Avenue Music.   www.DoctorMozart.com

1
C

Keyboard Cats

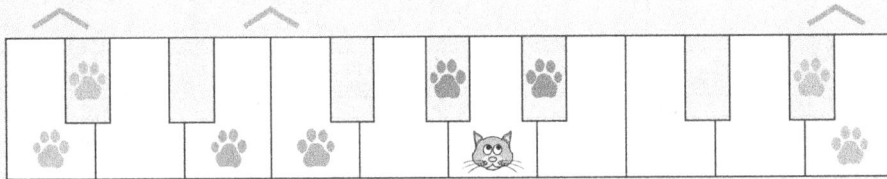

Draw a square bracket at each paw print pair.
Did Doctor Mozart step on any cats? __No__

I never step on cats.

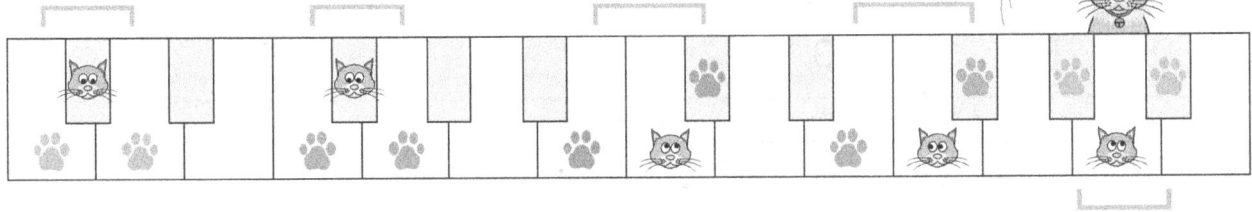

Doctor Mozart always steps *past* the cats.
But sometimes there are no cats. Write a V bracket
above each paw print pair that has *no* cat.

V bracket

Half Steps
No Cats

Whole Steps
Beware of Cats

Square bracket

Each paw print pair that has *no* cat is called a *half* step.
If there is no cat, the paw print pair is a ___half___ step.

Each paw print pair that *does* have a cat is called a *whole* step.
If there is a cat, the paw print pair is a ___whole___ step.

Here, Doctor Mozart stepped past some keys, as if they had invisible cats.
Write an X on each key he stepped past. Mark the whole steps with square brackets.

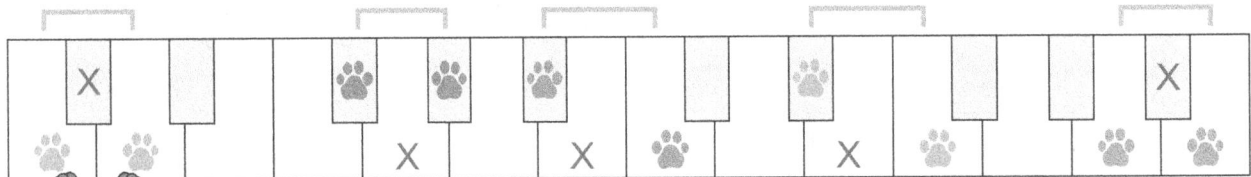

Invisible Cats

Draw lines to match these.

- Step past a cat ———————— • Whole step
- Don't step past a cat ———————— • Half step

What is the
difference
between a
whole step and
a half step?

Doctor Mozart Music Theory Workbook, Answers for Level 1 & OB. © MMVI, MMXVII Machiko and Paul Christopher Musgrave.   Published by April Avenue Music.   www.DoctorMozart.com

HaLF Steps & WHoLe Steps

Write an X on any keys that Doctor Mozart stepped past.

Draw brackets.

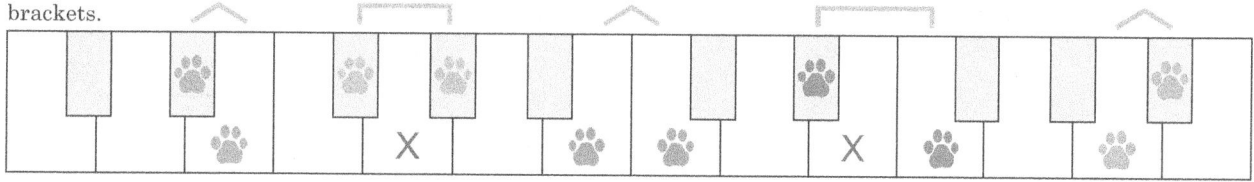

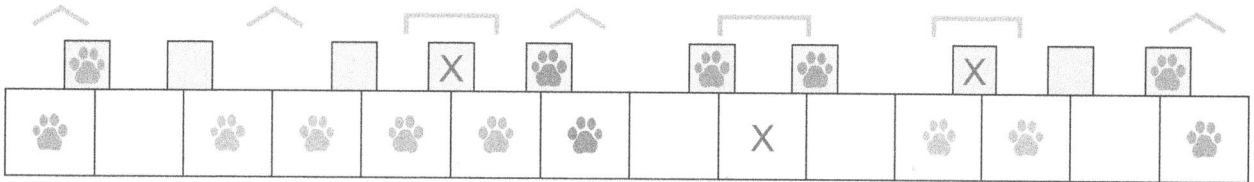

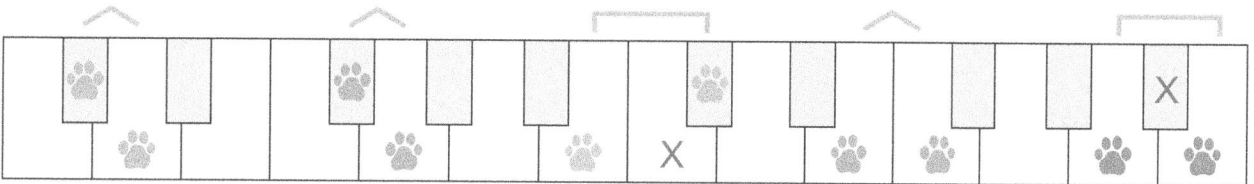

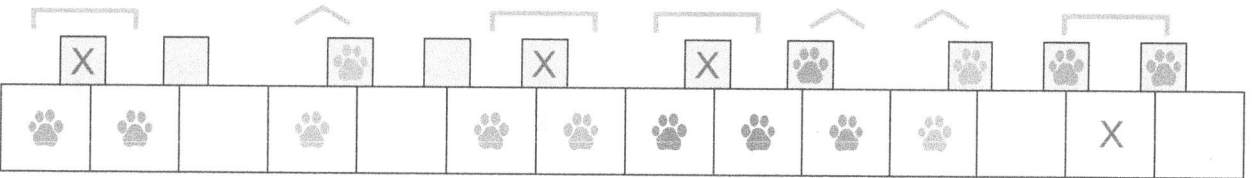

From each left paw print, draw a line to show a half step up.
Don't leave any space for cats!

Any space for me?

Left paw print   Left paw print

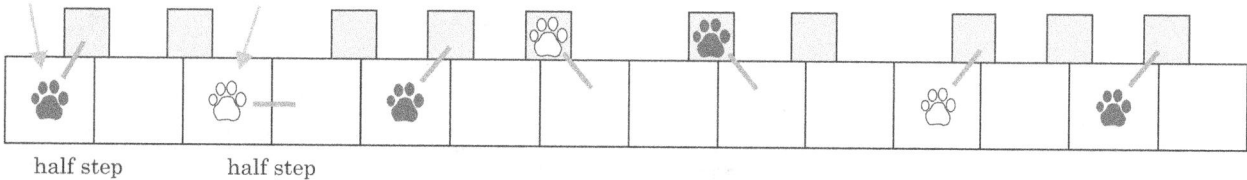

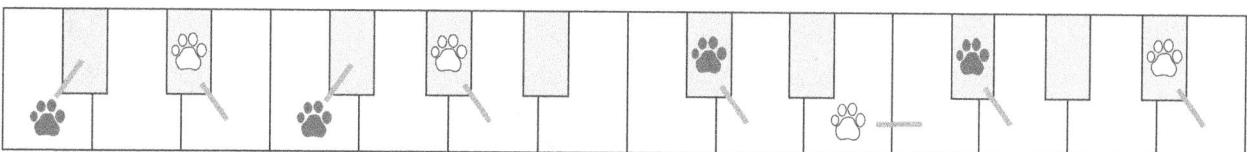

half step   half step

These are all left paw prints. For each, draw a line to show where his right paw should go.

1
C

Sharpen Up!

This is a **sharp** sign.
It means play the note
one half step higher.
The sign at left
is a __sharp__ sign.

Here is a normal F.

Here is an F *sharp*.

This black key is F sharp.

Trace the arrows.

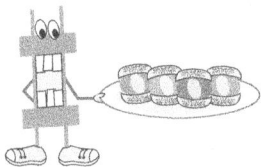

A sharp sign looks like the number sign on a telephone keypad.

Next, trace these sharps. Follow the arrows.
How many lines are needed to draw a sharp? __4__

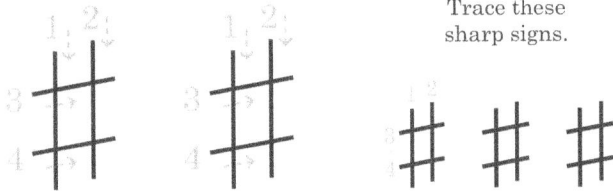

Trace these sharp signs.

Sharp signs are written *before* each note. But when we speak, we say "sharp" *after* the name of the note.

F sharp!

F sharp

Trace the arrows.

Look through the center of each sharp sign below.
If you see a *space*, then the sharp sign is for a *space* note.
If you see a *line*, then the sharp sign is for a *line* note.

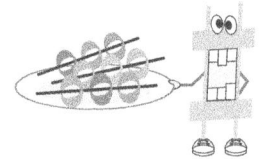

Trace. Write 3 more.

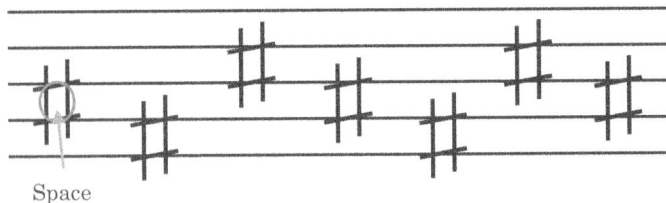

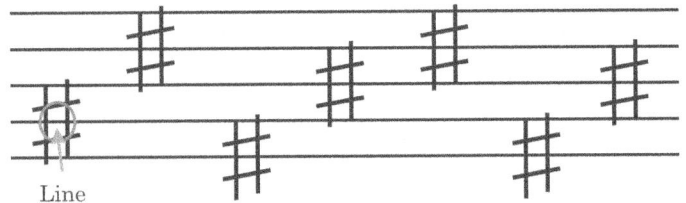

Space

Trace. Write 3 more.

Line

This is just one of several possible correct answers.

Are the above sharp signs for space notes
or line notes? __space notes__

Are the above sharp signs for space notes
or line notes? __line notes__

Doctor Mozart Music Theory Workbook, Answers for Level 1 & OB.   © MMVI, MMXVII Machiko and Paul Christopher Musgrave.   Published by April Avenue Music.   www.DoctorMozart.com

Sharpen Your Skill

Write a sharp sign in front of each note. Name each note.

F#   G#   G#   D#   A#   D#   C#

Next, from each paw print, draw a line to the key that is one half step higher. Name the black keys as sharps.

C#   D#   F#   G#   A#   C#   D#   F#   G#   A#

Here, circle any two paw prints that make a half step. Name all the paw print keys.

C C#   E F   A A#   D   E   G G#

C   D   E   F   G#   A#   C C#   E   F#   A A#

1
C

After each sharp sign, write the note that belongs to it. Name each note.

G#   D#   D#   F#   F#   G#   G#   A#   C#

SHARP WORK

Name the notes.

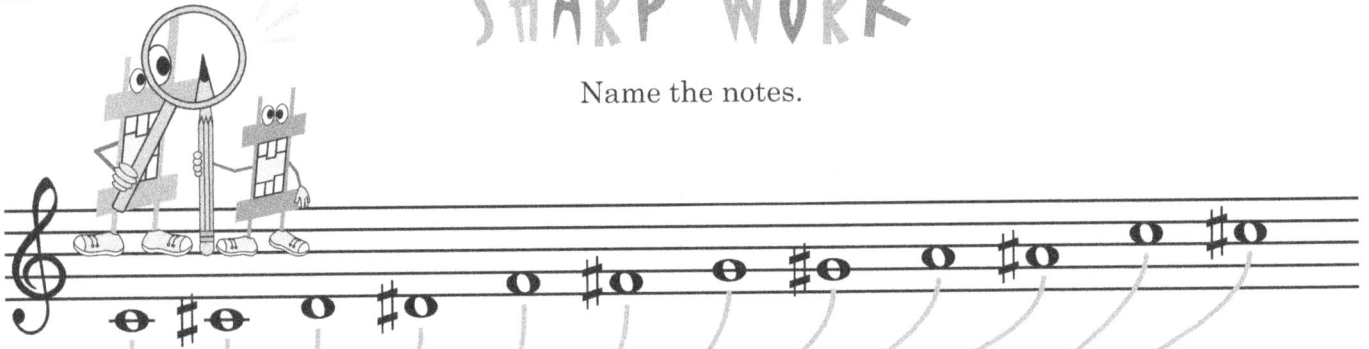

Draw
lines.

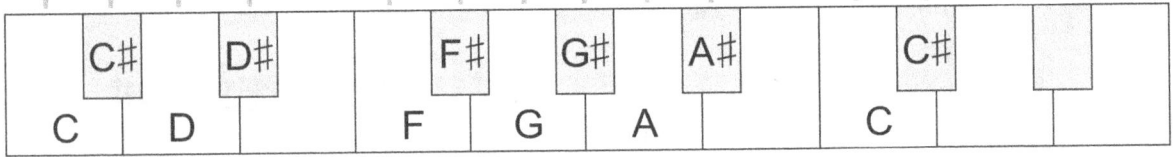

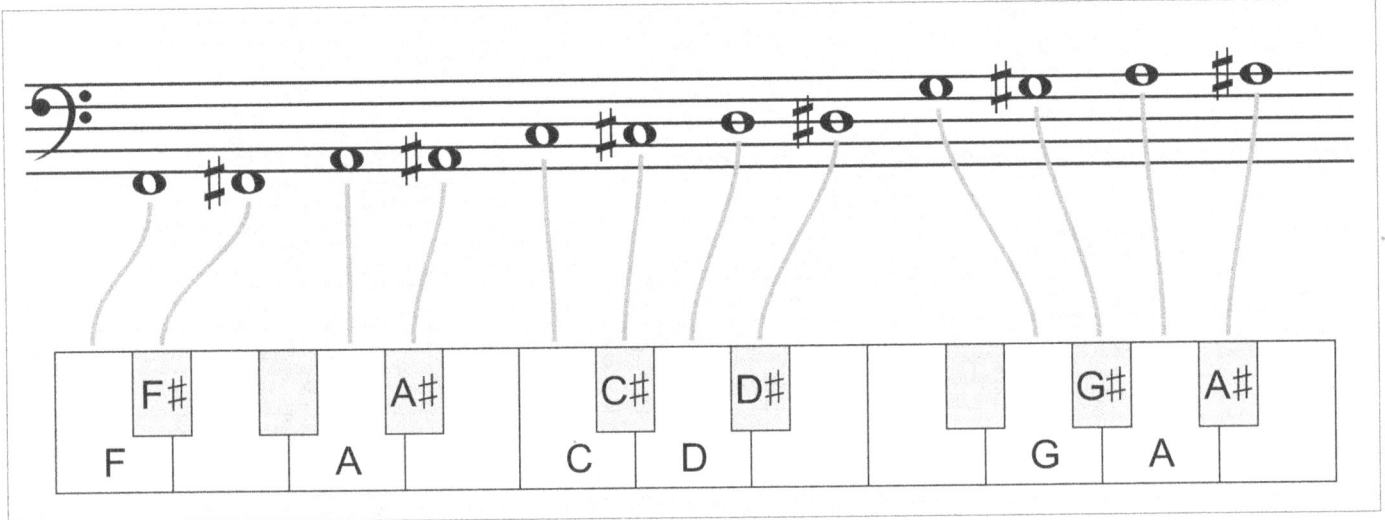

On the keyboard below, name
each black key as a sharp note.
Write it on the staff.

Make them sharp!

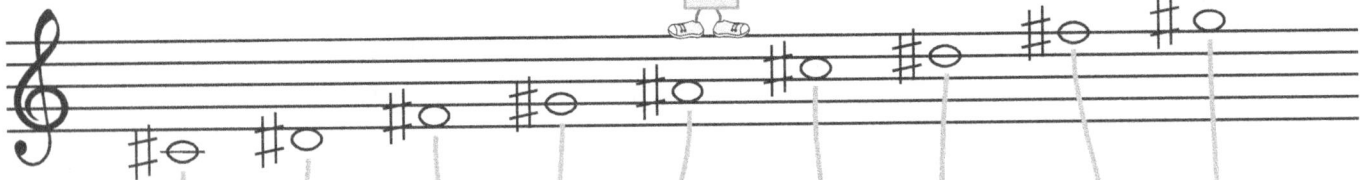

Draw
lines.

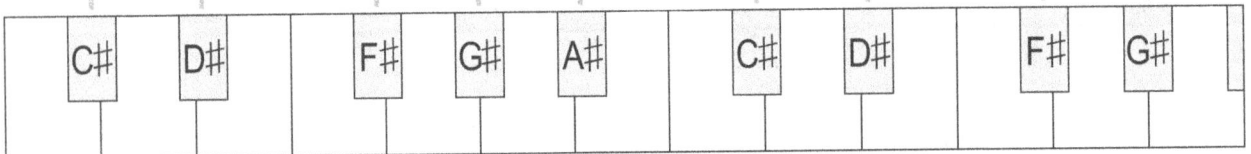

A Half Step Down

Now let's learn how to go *down* one half step. For each pair of paw prints, draw an arrow from the right paw print to the left.

half step   half step

How many of these half steps have 1 black key and 1 white key? **3**
How many have 2 white keys? **2** How many have 2 black keys? **0**

Next, from each right paw print, draw a line to the key that is one half step lower.

A half step up is the same distance as...

A half step down.

Another word
for *half step*
is *semitone*.

A half step *up* is the same distance as a half step ___**down**___.

Another word for *half step* is ___**semitone**___.

A half step is the smallest distance on the keyboard.

Below, draw a line from each paw print to the key that is one half step lower.

Doctor Mozart Music Theory Workbook, Answers for Level 1 & OB. © MMVI, MMXVII Machiko and Paul Christopher Musgrave. Published by April Avenue Music. www.DoctorMozart.com

Flatten Down

This is a **flat** sign.
It means play the note
one half step lower.
The sign at left is a
__flat__ sign.

A flat sign looks
similar to a lower
case letter **b**.

Here is a
normal B.

Here is a
B *flat*.

Trace the arrows.

Look at the numbers and arrows below.
How many lines and curves are needed
to draw a flat sign? __2__

Trace the
flat signs
at right.

Flat signs are written
before each note.
But when we speak,
we say "flat"*after*
the name of the note.

B flat

Trace the arrows.

B flat!

Line or
space?

Next, for each flat sign, write the matching note.

Trace.

Look here
for a line
or a space.

Draw lines.

Name
the
notes.

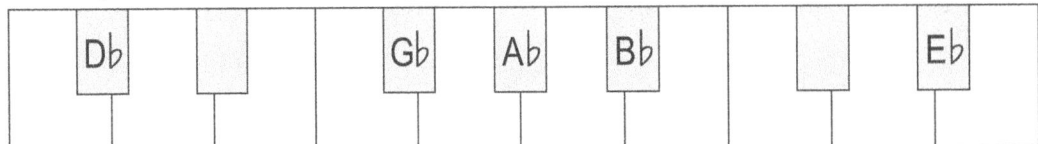

Db   Gb   Ab   Bb   Eb

Name the notes.

FLAT Friends

Draw lines.

Db	Eb		Gb	Ab			Db	Eb	
D	E		G	A			D	E	

Gb			Bb		Db	Eb		Gb			Bb	
G		B			D	E		G			B	

Next, write each paw print key on the staff. Write the white key first, then the black key. Use flats, not sharps.

Write each white key first.

Draw lines.

Write flats.

Sharps & Flats Quiz

Name the notes.

Draw lines.

Db		F#		Bb	C#	Eb		G#	
D		F		B	C	E		G	

	Ab		C#	Eb		G#	Bb		C#	
A		C		E		G	B	C	

Next, write these paw print keys on the staff. Both notes in each pair should have the same letter name.

Draw lines.

Doctor Mozart Music Theory Workbook, Answers for Level 1 & OB. © MMVI, MMXVII Machiko and Paul Christopher Musgrave.   Published by April Avenue Music.   www.DoctorMozart.com

Bar Lines Cancel Accidentals

A sharp or flat in front of a note is called an **accidental**. What is a flat or sharp in front of a note called? An _____accidental_____. An accidental can be a ___sharp___ or a ___flat___.

These three notes look the same, but one has a ___sharp___ sign in front. Circle the sharp sign.

A sharp is an accidental.

Does the sharp sign make just the first note sharp? Or does it make all three notes sharp?

The answer is:

The sharp sign makes all three notes sharp.

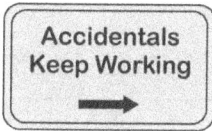

Accidentals Keep Working →

Why? Because accidentals keep working until the end of the bar. Accidentals keep working until the ___end___ of the ___bar___.

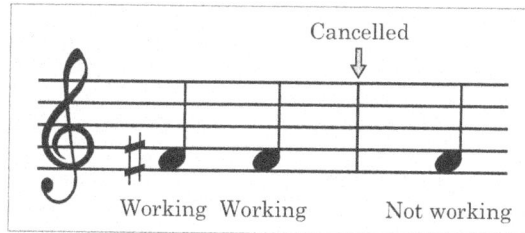

Cancelled

Working Working   Not working

Until the End of the Bar

1 C

A bar line always cancels any accidentals that have come before it. Bar lines always ___cancel___ accidentals.

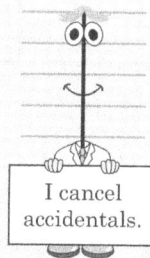

I cancel accidentals.

Every sharp keeps working until the ___end___ of the bar. Every flat keeps working until the end of the ___bar___.
Bar lines always ___cancel___ accidentals.

Below, trace the example. Then write the notes indicated. (That means write the notes shown.)

F♯ F♯ F♯   F♯ F♯ F♯   A♭ A♭ A♭   A♭ A♭ A♭

Just one sharp is needed!   Just one flat is needed!

To write the *same* F sharp three times in one bar, you need just ___1___ sharp sign.

Doctor Mozart Music Theory Workbook, Answers for Level 1 & OB. © MMVI, MMXVII Machiko and Paul Christopher Musgrave. Published by April Avenue Music. www.DoctorMozart.com

ACCIDENTAL CANCELLATION QUIZ

At right, why is the third F not sharp? Because it is *not* on the same line or space as the accidental. Accidentals work only on their own line or space.

Accidentals work only on their ___own___ line or space. Next, name these notes:

F♯   F♯   Not F♯

This sharp does not affect the top line.

Accidentals work only on their own line or space.

F♯   F   D♭   D♭   D   C♯   C♯   C♯   C   D♭   C♯   C

Trace.

Still D flat | Accidental cancelled | Still C sharp | Still C sharp | Accidental cancelled | Sharp | Not Sharp

D♭   D♭   G♭   G♭   G   A♭   A♭   A♯   A   G♭   G   G♭

Note: Real bars do not usually contain 4 whole notes.

Next, write the notes and accidentals indicated.*

* Write the notes *shown* by the alphabet letters.

C♯   F♯   C♯   C   F♯   F♯   F♯   B♭   B♭

Draw lines.

Bar lines cancel accidentals.

Here, write the notes and accidentals indicated.

F♯   F♯   G♯   G♯   A♯   A♯   A   D♭   D♭

Doctor Mozart Music Theory Workbook. Answers for Level 1 & OB.   © MMVI, MMXVII Machiko and Paul Christopher Musgrave.   Published by April Avenue Music.   www.DoctorMozart.com

Natural Signs Cancel Accidentals

This is a **natural** sign. It cancels any sharps and flats that have come before it on the same line or space. The sign at left is a ___natural___ sign.

Here, the natural sign cancels the flat.

Trace the arrows.

A natural sign looks like 2 Ls stuck together.

Here, the natural sign cancels the sharp.

Look at these natural signs. How many letter Ls are needed to draw a natural? __2__

Natural signs are written *before* each note. But when we speak, we say "natural" *after* the name of the note.

Trace these.

Trace these natural signs.

Trace the arrows.

B natural

B natural

After each natural sign, write the matching note.

Trace.

Look here for a line or a space.

Doctor Mozart Music Theory Workbook, Answers for Level 1 & OB. © MMVI, MMXVII Machiko and Paul Christopher Musgrave. Published by April Avenue Music. www.DoctorMozart.com

NATURAL PRACTICE

Name the notes.

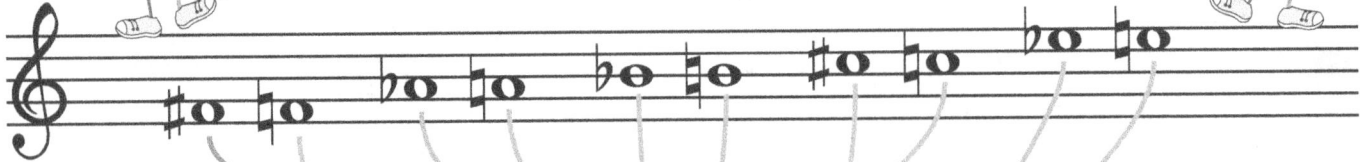

Draw lines.

F#	Ab	Bb		C#	Eb
F		A	B	C	E

Write each black key as a *sharp* note on the staff.
Beside it, write a *natural* note with the same name.

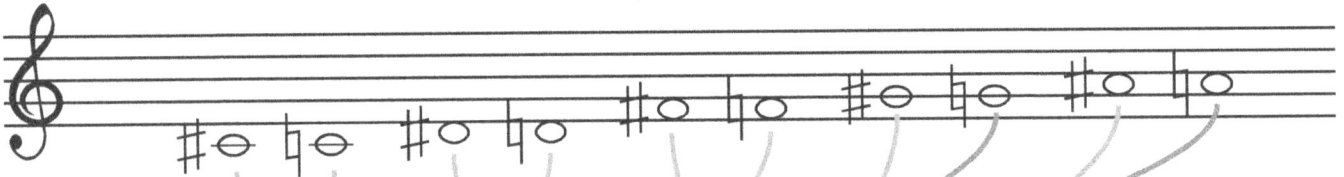

Write the sharp notes.

Write the natural notes too.

C#	D#		F#	G#	A#
C	D		F	G	A

Name the notes.

Repeat the above exercise, but this time, write *flat* and natural notes with the same name.

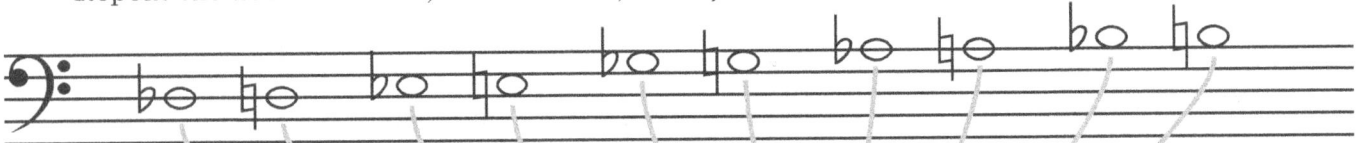

Db	Eb		Gb	Ab	Bb
	D	E		G	A	B

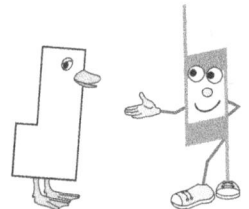

Doctor Mozart Music Theory Workbook, Answers for Level 1 & OB.   © MMVI, MMXVII Machiko and Paul Christopher Musgrave.   Published by April Avenue Music.   www.DoctorMozart.com

Accidental Quiz

Name the notes.

19

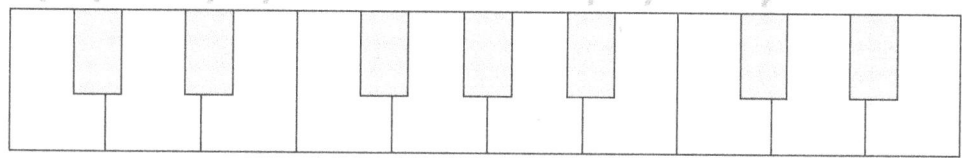

Draw lines.

Name them.

1
C

We both cancel accidentals, but in different ways.

Bar lines cancel *all* previous accidentals, no matter what line or space they are on. But *natural signs* work differently: They affect only their *own* line or space.

Name the notes.

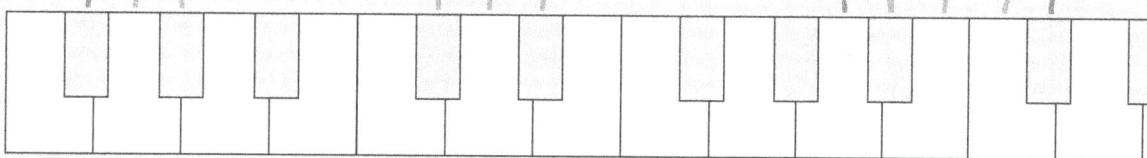

Draw lines.

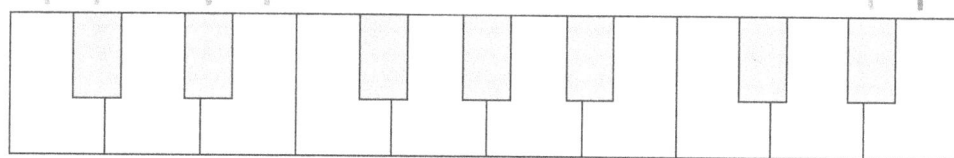

Doctor Mozart Music Theory Workbook, Answers for Level 1 & OB.   © MMVI, MMXVII Machiko and Paul Christopher Musgrave.   Published by April Avenue Music.   www.DoctorMozart.com

Every Black Key Has Two Names

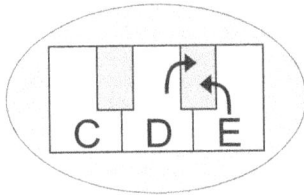

At left, name the white keys. Trace the arrows.

Are D♯ and E♭ played with the same key? __yes__

Notes like D♯ and E♭ are called **enharmonic notes**.

They have two different names, but we play them

with just one key on the keyboard. D♯ and E♭ are

called _____enharmonic_____ notes.

One key has 2 names.

C | D | E

I can be sharp or flat.

Name each black key two ways.

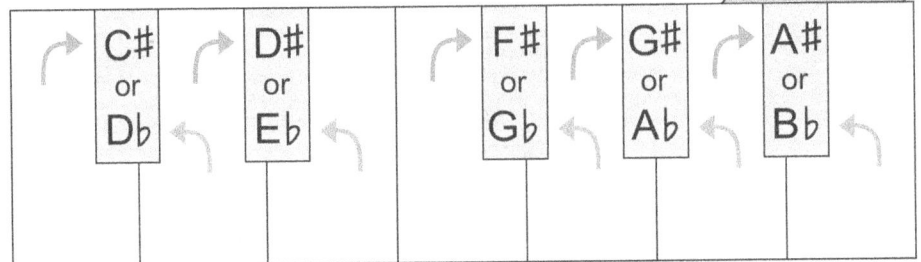

C# or Db | D# or Eb | F# or Gb | G# or Ab | A# or Bb

Enharmonic notes are written differently on the staff, but played with just one key on the keyboard.

Enharmonics

Write the enharmonic names for each black key.

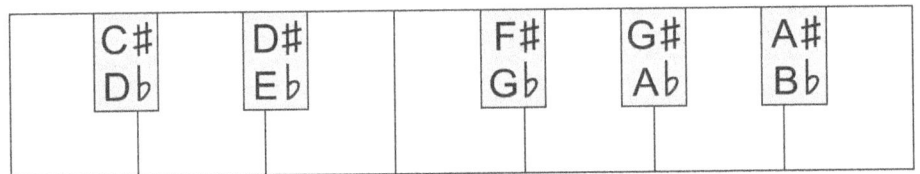

C# Db | D# Eb | F# Gb | G# Ab | A# Bb

Name these notes. Draw lines.

C#   Db   D#   Eb   F#   Gb   G#   Ab   A#   Bb

Write enharmonic
note pairs indicated
by the lines.

Enharmonic Quiz

Write the enharmonic name for each of these notes.

D♯	Eb	Ab	G♯	C♯	Db	Bb	A♯	G♯	Ab
A♯	Bb	Eb	D♯	F♯	Gb	Db	C♯	Gb	F♯

Draw lines to match the enharmonic notes.

1
C

Doctor Mozart Music Theory Workbook, Answers for Level 1 & OB. © MMVI, MMXVII Machiko and Paul Christopher Musgrave. Published by April Avenue Music. www.DoctorMozart.com

On the staff, write the two enharmonic notes for each black key. Name the notes.

Two names for each black key.

Draw lines.

C#	D#		F#	G#	A#
Db	Eb		Gb	Ab	Bb

Name the notes.

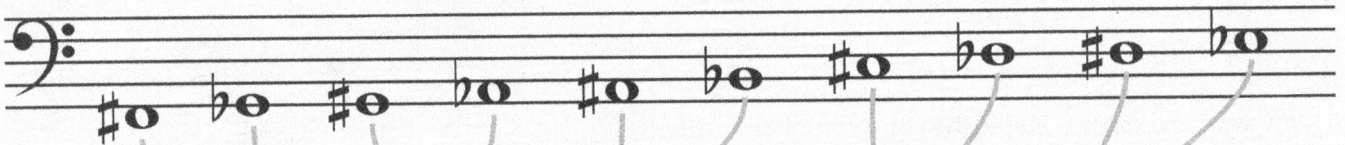

Draw lines.

F#	G#	A#		C#	D#
Gb	Ab	Bb		Db	Eb

Write a bass clef. Write 3 pairs of enharmonic notes.

Enharmonic notes.

Draw lines.
Name the notes.

This is just one of several possible correct answers.

F#		A#		D#
Gb		Bb		Eb

I have 2 names.

Doctor Mozart Music Theory Workbook, Answers for Level 1 & OB. © MMVI, MMXVII Machiko and Paul Christopher Musgrave. Published by April Avenue Music. www.DoctorMozart.com

ACCIDENTALS & ENHARMONICS Quiz

Name the notes.

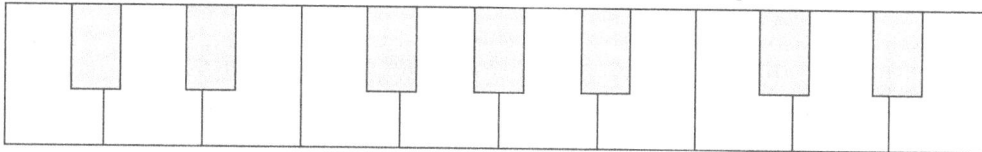

Eb D# Eb D#   E C# C C#   C Db C# C#

Draw lines.

Enharmonics

Bar lines cancel accidentals.

G Bb Bb   B C# C#   C F#   Gb   G A#   Bb

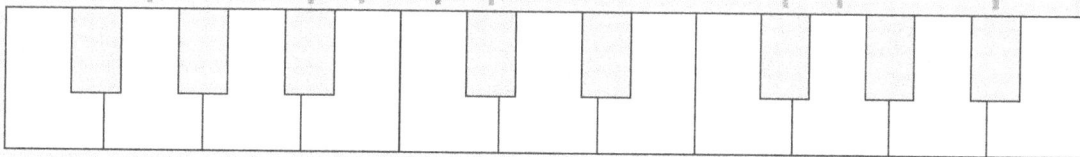

Enharmonic equivalent is another way of saying enharmonic note. Draw lines to match the enharmonic equivalent notes.

| C# | D# | | F# | G# | A# |

| Db | Eb | | Gb | Ab | Bb |

1 C

Doctor Mozart Music Theory Workbook. Answers for Level 1 & OB.   © MMVI, MMXVII Machiko and Paul Christopher Musgrave.   Published by April Avenue Music.   www.DoctorMozart.com

Chromatic?

For each paw print pair, name the white key first. Then use the *same* letter to name the black key.

These are chromatic semitones. Write them on the staff.

Same

Draw lines.

C   C#   F   F#   Bb   B   Eb   E

Use the *same* letter names.

C and C♯ make a *chromatic* semitone, because they are both named with the *same* alphabet letter. C and C♯ are a _____chromatic_____ semitone.

Or Diatonic?

This time, use two *different* letters to name each pair of notes.

Diatonic and *Different* both start with **D**.

These are diatonic semitones.

Different

Draw lines.

C   Db   F   Gb   A#   B   D#   E

Use *different* letter names.

C and D♭ make a _____diatonic_____ semitone. Each of the notes is named with a *different* letter.

In a chromatic semitone, both notes have the _____same_____ letter name. In a diatonic semitone, each note has a _____different_____ letter name. Next, write the semitones indicated.

Name the keys.

Draw lines.

C#   D   Gb   G   A   Bb   D   D#   F#   G

Look →   Diatonic   Chromatic   Diatonic   Chromatic   Diatonic

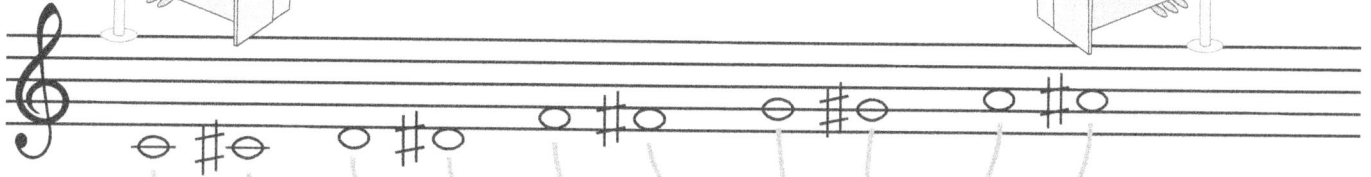

Chromatic or Diatonic ?

 **Same.** Chromatic

 **Different.** Diatonic

25

For each paw print key, write a note
on the staff. Then write a note that
is one *chromatic* half step higher.

Draw lines.

| C | C# | D | D# | | F | F# | G | G# | A | A# |

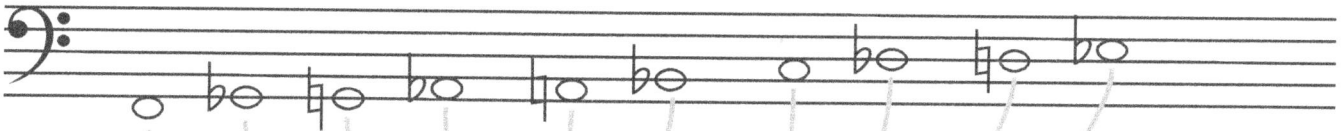

Now do the same, but with *diatonic* half steps.

Draw lines.

| F | Gb | G | Ab | A | Bb | | C | Db | D | Eb |

1
C

This is just one of several possible correct answers.

Write 3 chromatic and 3 diatonic half steps.

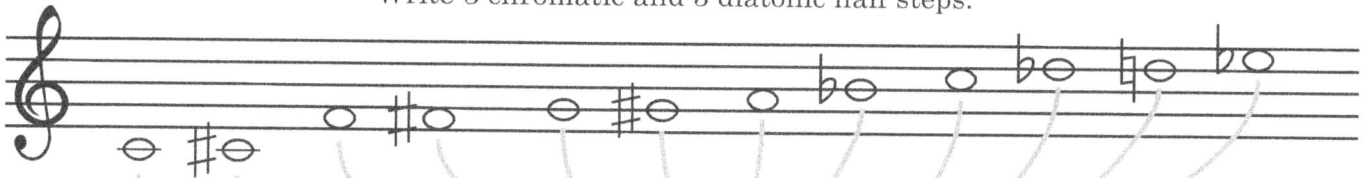

Draw lines.

 **Chromatic**

 **Diatonic**

| C | C# | | F | F# | G | G# | A | Bb | | C | Db | D | Eb |

CHROMATIC & DIATONIC QUIZ

For each paw print, write a note on the staff.
Then write a note that is one *chromatic* half step lower.

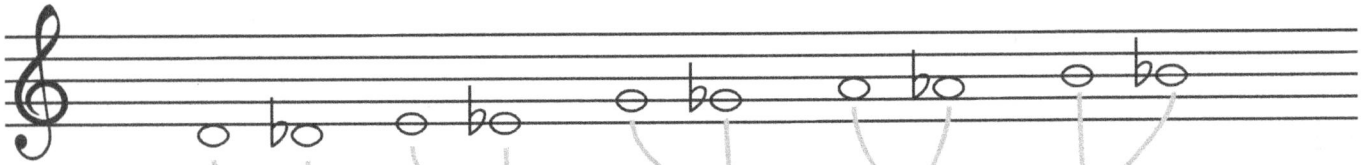

Draw lines.

 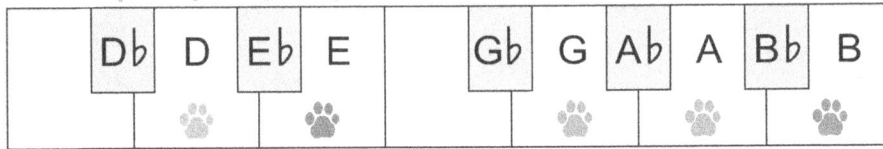

Now do the same, but with *diatonic* half steps.

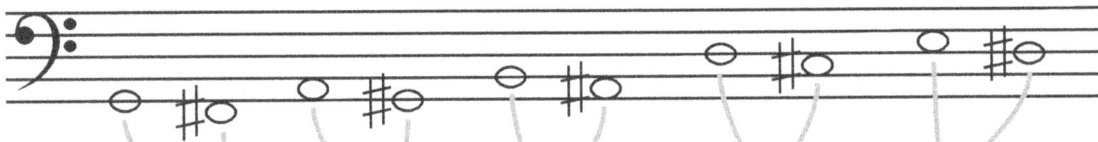

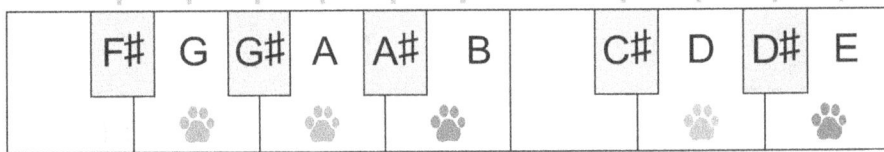 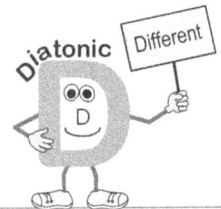

Write 3 chromatic and 3 diatonic half steps. Make them go down, not up.

This is just one of several possible correct answers.

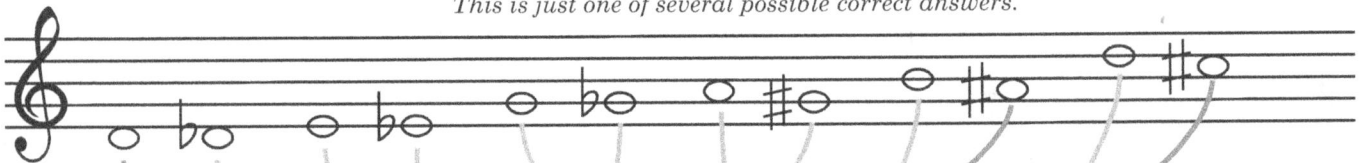

Go down.

 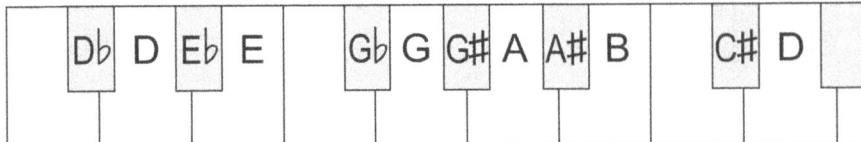 

Draw lines.

Chromatic or Diatonic?

Accidental

Write any 8 black key notes you like.

This is just one of several possible correct answers.

Draw
lines.

Write 2 diatonic half steps and 2 chromatic half steps.

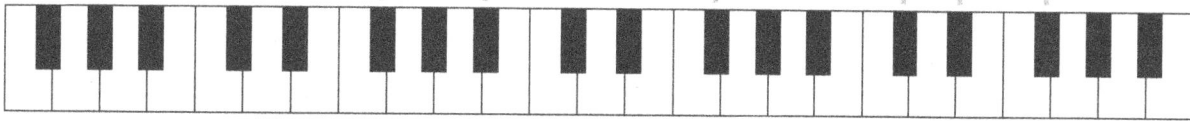

Draw
lines.

This is just one of many possible correct answers.

Next, mark each chromatic half step with a curved bracket.
Mark each diatonic half step with a V bracket.

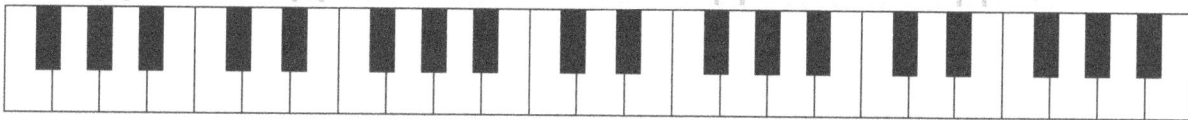

Draw lines.

V bracket

Curved bracket

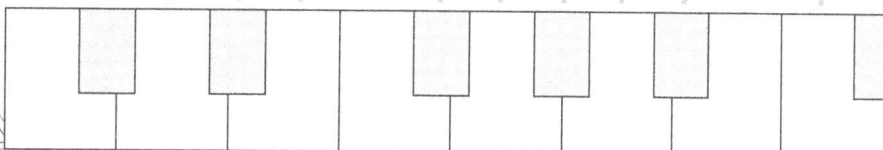
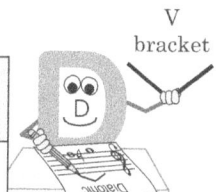

Half Steps & Half Notes

Add the length of these notes and rests. Write the sums in the boxes.

A quarter rest has the same length as a quarter note.

A half rest has the same length as a half note.

A whole rest has the same length as a whole note.

♩ + 𝄽 = **2**   𝄼 + ♩ = **4**

𝄻 + 𝄽 + ♩ = **7**   ♩ + ♩ + 𝄽 = **4**   ♩ + 𝄼 + 𝄼 = **8**

Write accidentals to make as many half steps as possible.

This is one of several possible correct answers.

Draw lines.

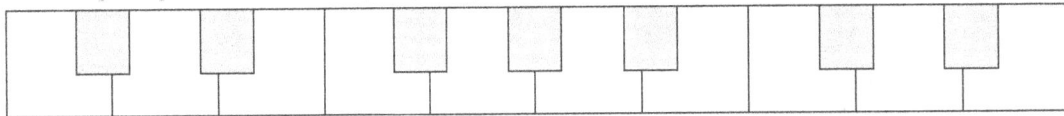

Next, write some chromatic and diatonic half steps. Use half notes and quarter notes.

Be creative!

Number the beats.   1   2   3   4   1   2   3   4   1   2   3   4

Draw lines.

This is just one of many possible correct answers.

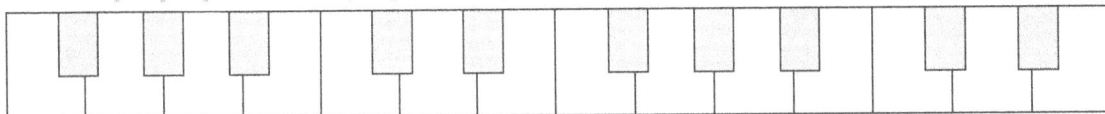

TEMPO
TERMINOLOGY REVIEW

Write the correct tempo term in each box.

CHEETAH

as fast as possible
Prestissimo

very fast
Presto

fast
Allegro

a little slower than allegro
Allegretto

at a moderate tempo
Moderato

a little faster than andante
Andantino

at a slow walking pace
Andante

slower than andante
Adagio

SLOTH

a little faster than largo
Larghetto

very slow
Largo
Lento

1
C

Speak Italian!

vivace
Lively or brisk.

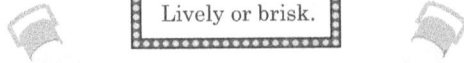

vee-VAH-che

Slow down gradually.

Slow Down

ritardando (rit.)

or **rallentando (rall.)**

cantabile
Play as if singing.

kun-TAH-bee-le

marcato (marc.)
Emphasize each note.

mar-KUH-to

Quiz

Draw lines to match each musical term with its meaning.

dolce — majestic

maestoso — gently & smoothly

marcato — gradually speed up

accelerando — emphasize each note

cantabile — gradually slow down

rallentando — in a singing style

ritardando — lively or brisk

grazioso — graceful

vivace

tempoI
or **tempo primo**
or **a tempo**
Play in the original tempo.

Gradually get faster.

accelerando
(accel.)

ah-che-le-RAHN-do

grazioso
Play gracefully.

grat-see-OH-zo

dolce
Smoothly & gently.

DOL-che

maestoso
Play or sing majestically.

my-STOW-zo

Doctor Mozart Music Theory Workbook, Answers for Level 1 & OB.   © MMVI, MMXVII Machiko and Paul Christopher Musgrave.   Published by April Avenue Music.   www.DoctorMozart.com

Write one Italian term for each definition. The terms you need are in the yellow box.

Very slow	lento or largo
A little faster than largo	larghetto
Slower than andante	adagio
Slow, at a walking pace	andante
A little faster than andante	andantino
At a moderate tempo	moderato
A little slower than allegro	allegretto
Lively or brisk	vivace
Fast	allegro
Very fast	presto
As fast as possible	prestissimo
Smoothly and gently	dolce

Spell carefully!

Use these terms.

a tempo
accelerando
adagio
allegretto
allegro
andante
andantino
cantabile

dolce
grazioso
larghetto
legato
lento or largo
maestoso
marcato
moderato

molto
poco
prestissimo
presto
rallentando
staccato
vivace

Gradually speed up	accelerando
Gradually slow down	rallentando
Original tempo	a tempo
Majestically	maestoso
Gracefully	grazioso
Emphasize each note	marcato
In a singing style	cantabile
A lot	molto
A little	poco
Let go immediately	staccato
Join the notes	legato

1
C

Tempo Test

Write the tempo terms.

as fast as possible	prestissimo	a little faster than andante	andantino
very fast	presto	at a slow walking pace	andante
fast	allegro	slower than andante	adagio
a little slower than allegro	allegretto	a little faster than largo	larghetto
at a moderate tempo	moderato	very slow	lento or largo

Doctor Mozart Music Theory Workbook, Answers for Level 1 & OB. ©MMVI, MMXVII Machiko and Paul Christopher Musgrave.   Published by April Avenue Music.   www.DoctorMozart.com

Key Signatures

Here are two key signatures.

G major key signature

Trace.

In the key of G major, every F should be sharp.

In the key of F major, every B should be flat.

Sharp name: **F#**
This key signature is for **G** major.

Bar lines do *not* cancel key signatures.

F major key signature

Trace.

Flat name: **B♭**
This key signature is for **F** major.

Here is some music written twice—once with accidentals, and once with a key signature.
Trace the key signature. Circle all the notes that should be played with black keys.

Written with accidentals

Written with a key signature

Draw an arrow to the grand staff that has fewer sharp signs.

Circle the flat notes.

Written with accidentals

Trace.

Written with a key signature

Draw an arrow to the grand staff that has fewer flat signs.

Doctor Mozart Music Theory Workbook, Answers for Level 1 & OB. © MMVI, MMXVII Machiko and Paul Christopher Musgrave.   Published by April Avenue Music.   www.DoctorMozart.com

What is a Scale?

Trace this G major key signature.
Circle each note that should be played with a black key.

Draw a V bracket at each half step.

Each G major scale starts and ends on G.

Draw lines.

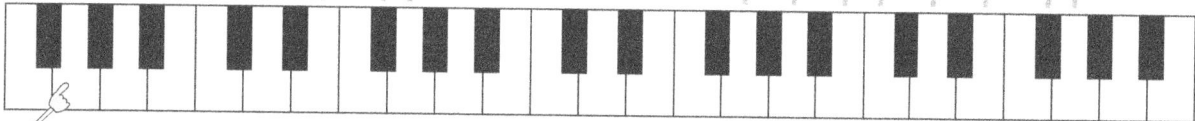

What is the first note of each G major scale? __G__ And the last note? __G__

Do the same with these two F major scales.

Each F major scale starts and ends on F.

Draw lines.

What is the first note of each F major scale? __F__ And the last note? __F__

Next, after each clef, write an F major key signature and scale. Circle each note that should be played with a black key. Draw a V bracket at each half step.

Doctor Mozart Music Theory Workbook, Answers for Level 1 & OB. © MMVI, MMXVII Machiko and Paul Christopher Musgrave. Published by April Avenue Music. www.DoctorMozart.com

1 C

Ties Are Not Slurs

Tie

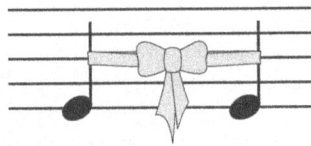

A tie joins two notes on the *same* line or space.

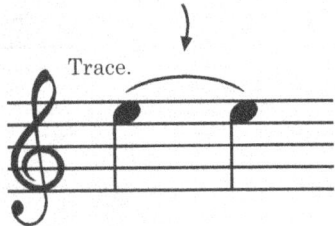

Trace.

Play only the first note, and hold it for the length of both notes.

A tie is a curve that connects two notes that are on the **same** line or space. Play only the first note, and hold it for the length of **both** notes. Do not play the second note!

How should you play tied notes?

Play this note, and hold for two beats.   Don't play this note. Just hold.

Circle every note that should be played. Do not circle the second note of any ties.

How can you tie more than two notes? Use a separate tie sign for each pair of notes. Trace these ties.

Count: 1   2   3   4

Play this note → and hold for 4 beats.

Slur

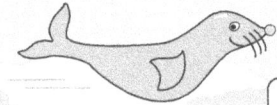

Play them legato.

A slur can join *two* notes that are on *different* lines or spaces.   A slur can also join *more than two* notes. Play all the notes legato.

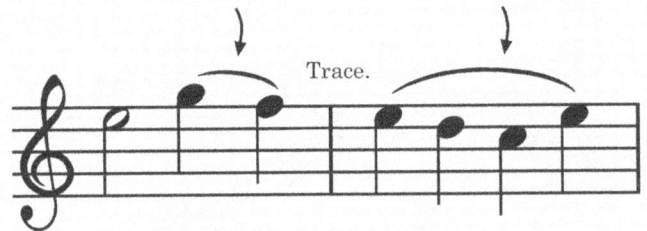

Trace.

Play slurred notes legato.

A slur connects notes on **different** lines or spaces. Play all slurred notes, and play them **legato**.

Rests are never slurred or tied.

Write *tie* or *slur* on each blank.

slur   tie   slur

slur   tie   tie

This is just one of many possible correct answers:
Write some tied notes and slurred notes.

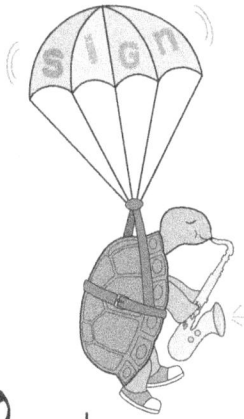

Expert sign Test

Name the musical sign at each blue arrow.
Use the list to help you remember.

accent
crescendo
diminuendo
double bar line
fermata
flat
forte
fortissimo
mezzo forte
mezzo piano
natural
pianissimo
piano
repeat sign
sharp
slur
staccato
tie
time signature

tie   slur   repeat sign

slur   staccato   **ff** fortissimo

sharp   natural   mezzo piano   **mp**

time signature   crescendo   diminuendo or decrescendo

mezzo forte   **mf**   **p** piano   fermata

f forte   accent   flat   slur   tie   **pp** pianissimo   double bar line

---

For how many quarter note beats
should each pair of tied notes be held?

2   3

4   5

Draw lines to match *opposite* meanings.

p   **pp**

staccato   crescendo

ff   **f**

diminuendo   legato

1
C

Write the clefs. Trace and name each key signature.

MULTI QUIZ

On the staff, circle each note that is played with a black key.

_G_ major
Sharp name: **F#**

Write the scale in both staffs.

_F_ major
Flat name: **B♭**

Write the scale in both staffs.

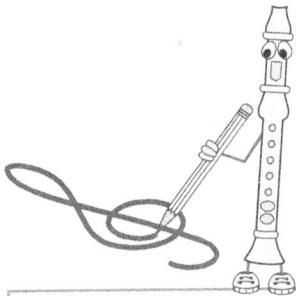

Look at how each note is named.
Then write the correct clef.

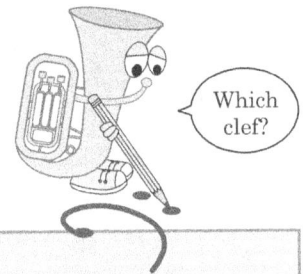

Which clef?

C	C	B	B
E	E	D	D
A	A	F	F

  **REVIEW**

Name these key signatures.

C Major   C Major   G Major   G Major   F Major   F Major

Write the correct clef for each key signature. Name the key signatures.

G Major   F Major   G Major   F Major   G Major   G Major

Write these key signatures.

F Major   C Major   G Major   F Major   C Major   G Major

Expert Exam

 Tie or... Slur?

Write *tie* or *slur* on each blank.

slur   tie   tie   slur   slur   slur

Next, write the notes indicated. Remember, accidentals keep working until the end of the bar.

Bb   Bb   A#   A#   Db   A#   A   Gb   Gb

PRO EXAM

Write the correct sign or note in each box.

3/4 time signature	4/4 time signature	accent	bass clef	crescendo
3/4	4	>	𝄢	<
diminuendo	**fermata**	**flat**	**forte**	**fortissimo**
>	𝄐	♭	f	ff
half note	**half rest**	**mezzo forte**	**mezzo piano**	**natural**
♩	▬	mf	mp	♮
pianissimo	**piano**	**quarter note**		
pp	p	♩		
quarter rest	**sharp**	**staccato**		
𝄽	♯	♩•		
treble clef	**whole note**	**whole rest**		
𝄞	o	▬		

In this book, you have learned about accidentals, diatonic and chromatic half steps, enharmonic notes, scales, key signatures, musical terms, slurs, and ties. Good job!

Compose Your Own Music

Write a grand staff and a time signature.
Write any notes and rests you like.
Use some marks from the top of this page.

There are many possible answers. However, be sure the number of beats in each bar matches the time signature, and that the note stems go in the right direction, etc.

Number the beats.   1   1

Doctor Mozart® Music Theory Workbook

In-Depth Piano Theory Fun for Children's Music Lessons and Home Schooling

> We will help you understand and remember each lesson.

Older Beginners

> Hi! I'm Doctor Mozart.

Highly effective for beginners learning a musical instrument.

Doctor Mozart workbooks are filled with friendly cartoon characters. They make it fun to learn music theory in-depth. And in-depth music theory knowledge is essential for children learning a musical instrument. Use Doctor Mozart workbooks by themselves or with other teaching materials. Use them for music lessons and for home schooling.

The authors, Machiko and Paul Musgrave, are both graduates of Juilliard. Machiko has taught piano and theory at Soai University in Japan. Paul is an Associate of the Royal Conservatory of Music. The authors hope you enjoy using this book!

OB

Many thanks to Kevin Musgrave for his meticulous proof-reading and insightful suggestions.
Created by Machiko and Paul Christopher Musgrave. Illustrated by Machiko Yamane Musgrave.   1.0.4

Doctor Mozart Music Theory Workbook, Answers for Level 1 & OB.   © MMVI, MMXVII Machiko and Paul Christopher Musgrave.   Published by April Avenue Music.   www.DoctorMozart.com

Meet the Keyboard

Knowing music theory helps me play the piano better.

The better I know music theory, the faster and better I can learn each new piece of music.

Let's learn music theory together. It's fun!

On this keyboard, circle all the groups of 3 black keys.

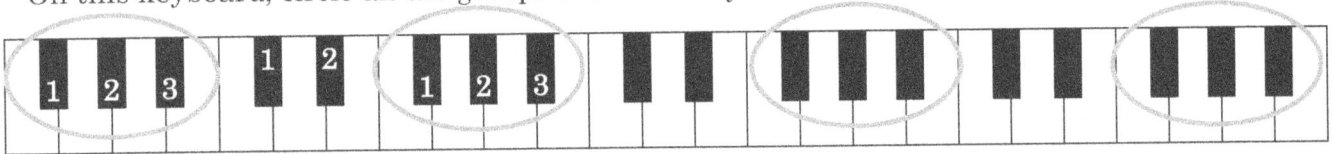

Keyboards always have black keys in groups of 2 and 3. Circle any mistakes on these keyboards.

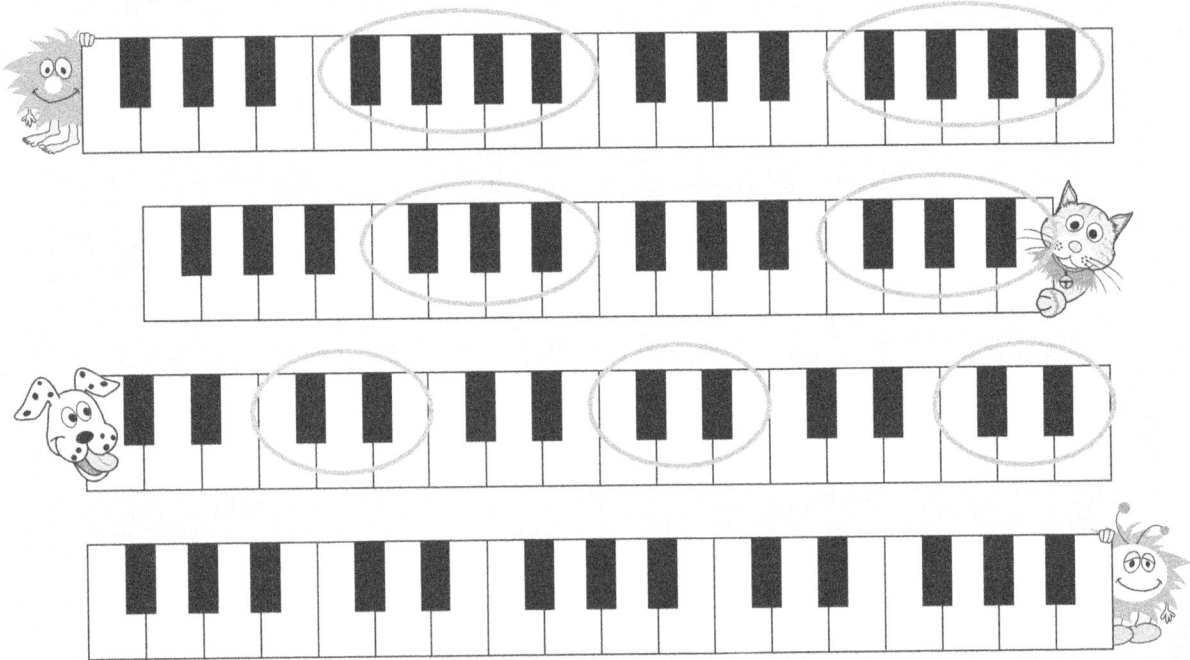

Write a check mark in the box beside each correct answer.

Black keys should be in groups of		The order of the groups should be	
2 and 4	☐	3 2 2 3	☐
3 and 4	☐	2 3 5 2	☐
2 and 3	✔	2 3 2 3	✔
5 and 3	☐	any order is fine.	☐

The Music Alphabet

3

Circle all the Ds on this keyboard. Number the black keys. Is there any key named H? __No__

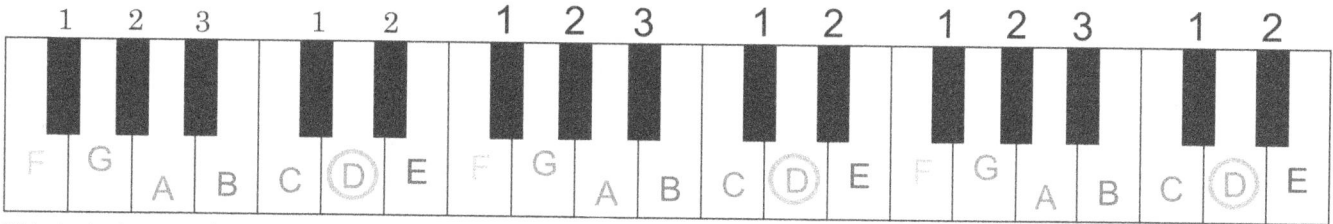

This is the lower end of the keyboard.

This is the higher end.

What 7 letters are used for piano keys? __A B C D E F G__   What letter comes after G? __A__

Each group of 2 black keys has D in the middle.

Within every group of two black keys, there is a note named __D__.

D is also between C and E.

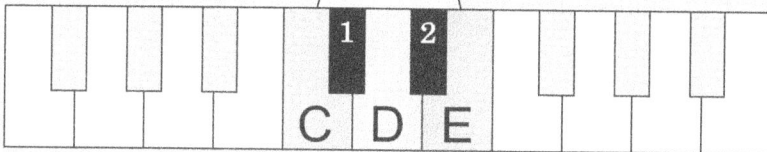

Trace the letters

Next, number the black keys. Name all the colored keys.

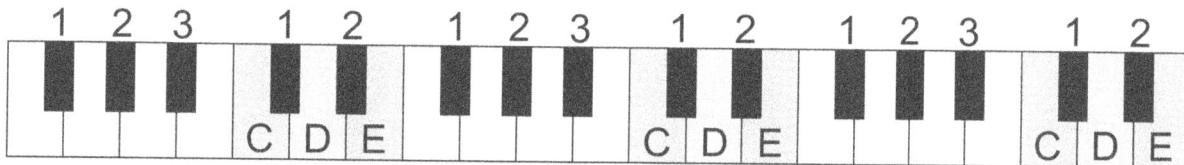

Each group of 3 black keys has G and A in the middle.

What 2 notes are inside every group of 3 black keys? __G__ and __A__

Trace the letters

Name all the colored keys.

O B

Doctor Mozart Music Theory Workbook, Answers for Level 1 & OB.   © MMVI, MMXVII Machiko and Paul Christopher Musgrave.   Published by April Avenue Music.   www.DoctorMozart.com

A Step or a Skip?

Trace the gray letters and brackets.

Are F and G neighbors? **Yes**
F and G make a **step**.
Any two white keys that are
neighbors make a ___ **step** ___.

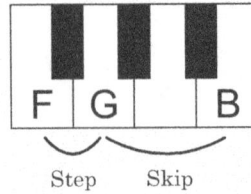

F   G   B

Step   Skip

Are G and B neighbors? **No**.
G and B make a **skip**.
Any two white keys that are
not neighbors make a ___ **skip** ___.

Name the colored keys. Trace the brackets. Write *step* or *skip* under each bracket.

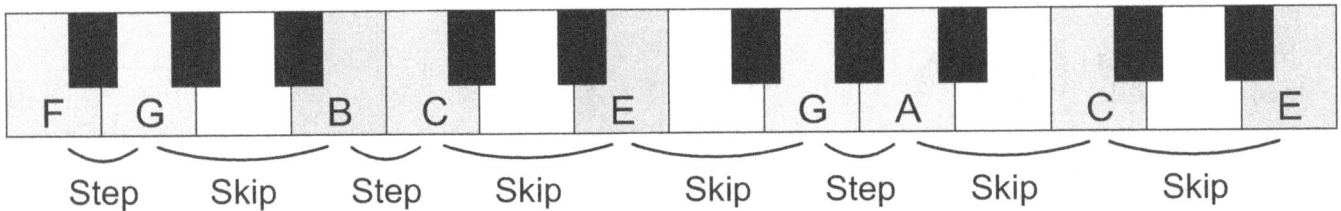

F G   B C   E   G A   C   E

Step   Skip   Step   Skip   Skip   Step   Skip   Skip

Circle each pair of letters
that makes a step:

(BC) CE (FG) FA BD (GA)

Circle each pair of letters
that makes a skip:

(AC) GA (CD) EF (GB) (DF)

For each colored key, name the white keys that are one step higher, and one step lower.

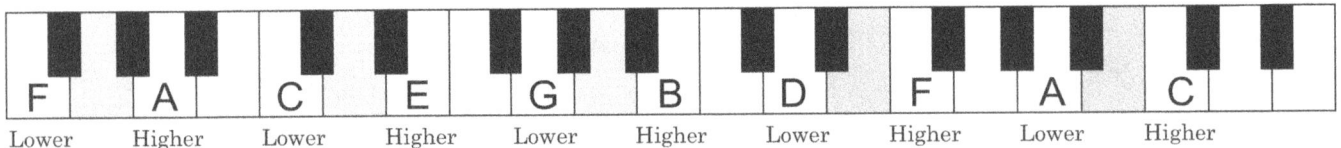

F   A   C   E   G   B   D   F   A   C

Lower Higher Lower Higher Lower Higher Lower Higher Lower Higher

---

Name the 2 white keys that
make each step or skip.

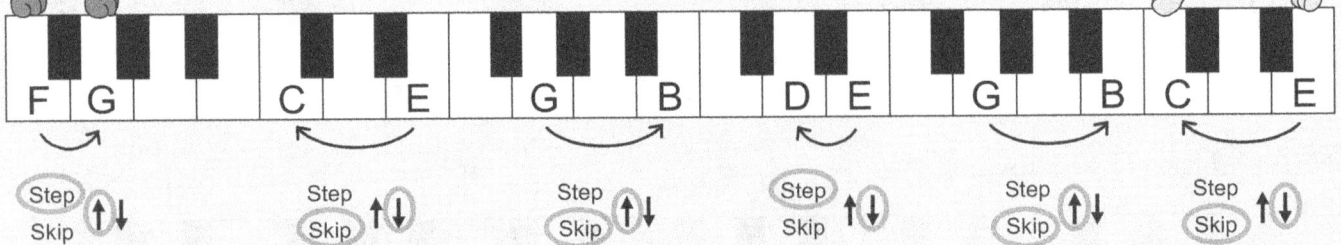

F G   C   E   G   B   D E   G   B   C   E

Step
Skip ↑↓

Step
Skip ↑↓

Step
Skip ↑↓

Step
Skip ↑↓

Step
Skip ↑↓

Step
Skip ↑↓

Circle the correct words and arrows.

A Staff is Like a Ladder for Notes

Trace these lines and numbers.

5 ————————————
4 ————————————
3 ————————————
2 ————————————
1 ————————————

4 ————————————
3 ————————————
2 ————————————
1 ————————————

These 5 lines are a *staff*.

A staff has **5** lines and **4** spaces.

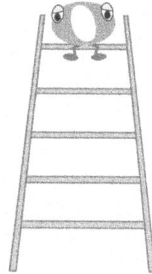
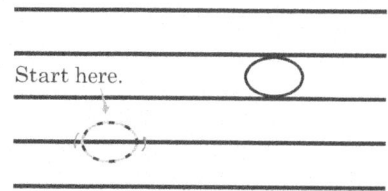

Here are some notes on a staff.
They are ovals, not circles. Trace them.

This note is higher.

Start here.

This note is lower.

A staff is like a ladder for ___ **notes** ___.

Trace these notes.

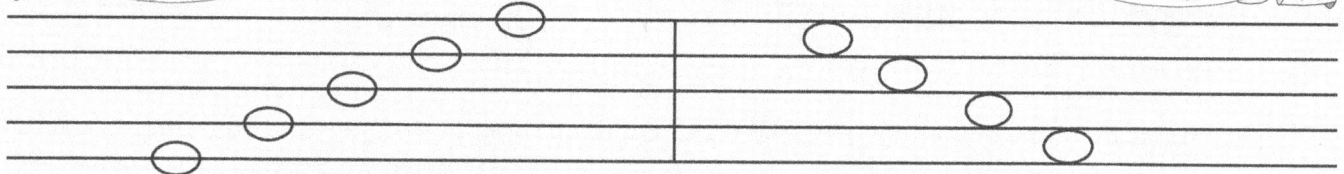

line notes.

space notes.

These are *line* notes going *up*.
True or false? __ **true** __

These are *space* notes going *down*.
True or false? __ **true** __

Write the line number for each note.

Which line?
Which space?

Trace the notes.

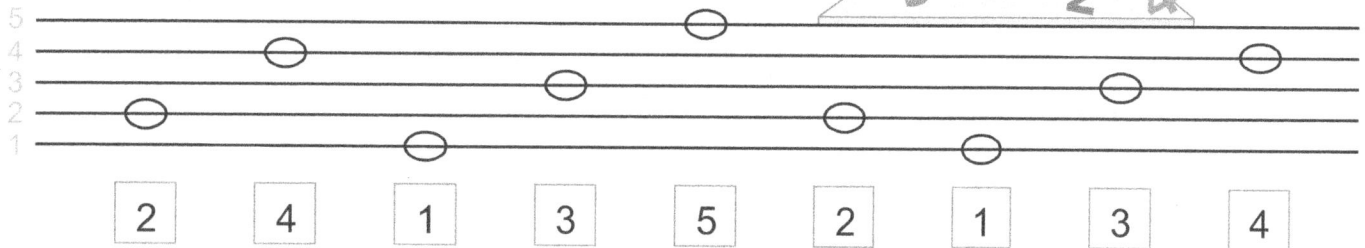

| 2 | 4 | 1 | 3 | 5 | 2 | 1 | 3 | 4 |

Write the space number for each note.

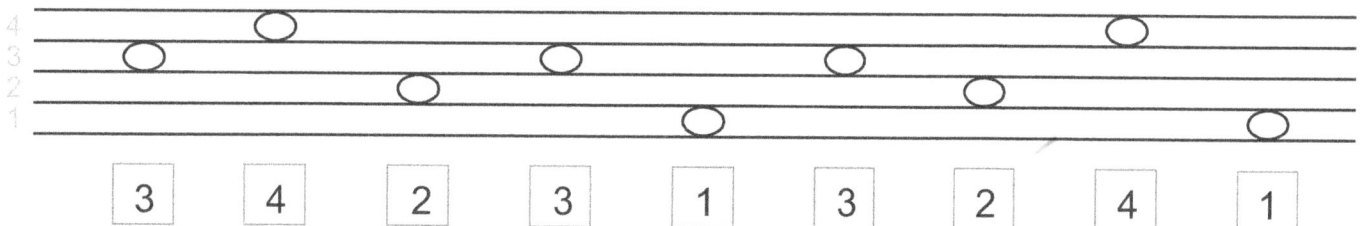

| 3 | 4 | 2 | 3 | 1 | 3 | 2 | 4 | 1 |

O
B

Staff Code Quiz

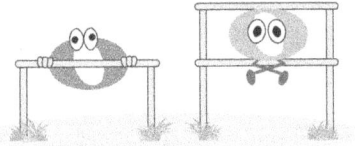

Write the correct note above each box.

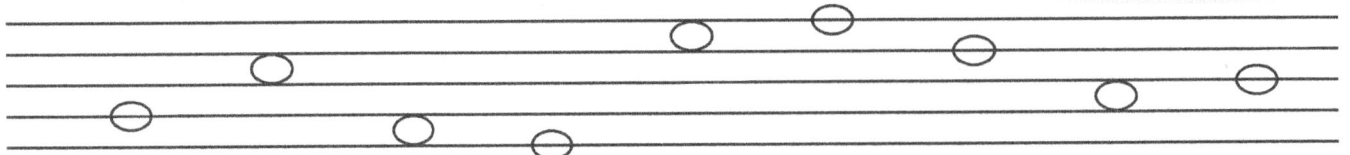

2L	3S	1S	1L	4S	5L	4L	2S	3L
2nd Line	3rd Space							

Trace each note. Write its code in the box below it.

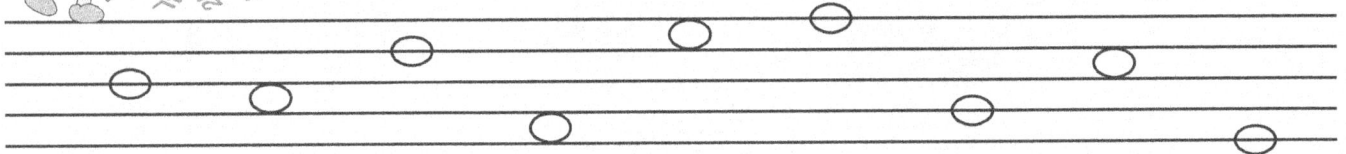

3L	2S	4L	1S	4S	5L	2L	3S	1L

What do steps and skips look like on the staff? Trace these notes and find out.

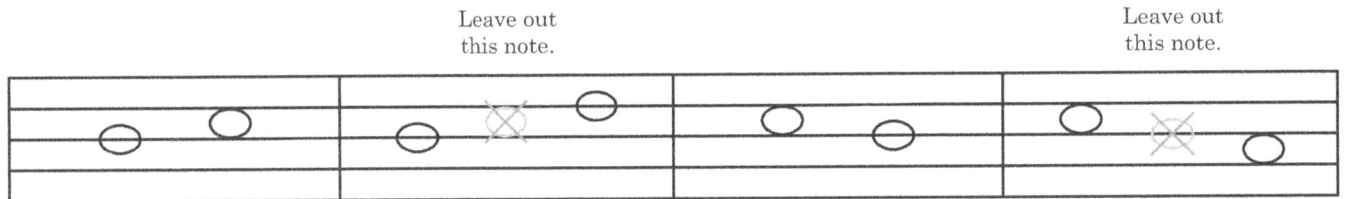

Leave out this note.   Leave out this note.

Step up   *Skip* up   Step down   *Skip* down

Circle the correct words and arrows.

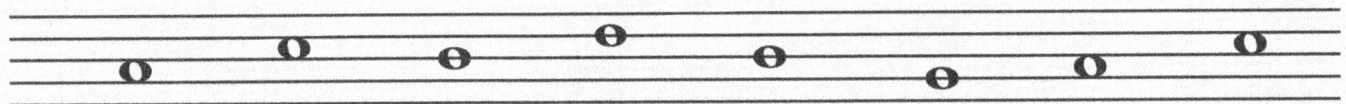

Step/Skip ↑↓   Step/Skip ↑↓   Step/Skip ↑↓   Step/Skip ↑↓   Step/Skip ↑↓   Step/Skip ↑↓   Step/Skip ↑↓

Write steps and skips on the staff, as shown.

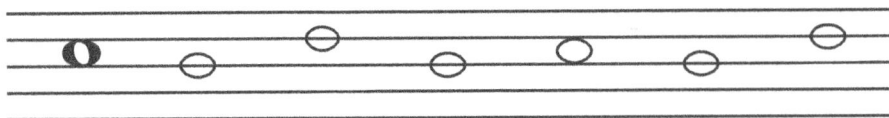

Step   Skip

Step	Skip	Skip	Step	Step	Skip
↓	↑	↓	↑	↓	↑

The Clefs: Bass and Treble

Here are two musical signs, which we call clefs.

The bass clef is for lower notes.

The treble clef is for higher notes.

Trace the brackets.

Low notes

High notes

Middle C is a special note near the middle of your keyboard.

The special C near the middle of your keyboard is called __middle__ C.

The __bass__ clef is for __lower__ notes.   The __treble__ clef is for __higher__ notes.

Trace these treble clefs. Color the G line green. Write 2 treble clefs on your own.

This is the G line.

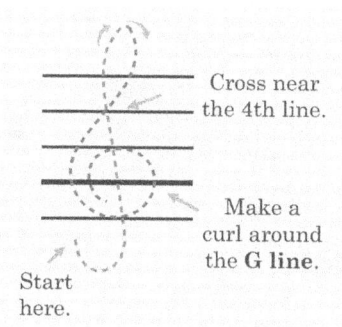

Cross near the 4th line.

Make a curl around the **G line**.

Start here.

Trace these bass clefs. Color the F line yellow. Write 2 bass clefs on your own.

O
B

Start at the **F line**.

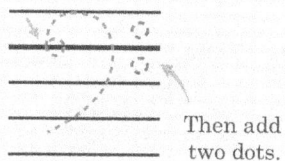

This is the F line.

Then add two dots.

Doctor Mozart Music Theory Workbook, Answers for Level 1 & OB.   © MMVI. MMXVII Machiko and Paul Christopher Musgrave.   Published by April Avenue Music.   www.DoctorMozart.com

Middle C on the Grand Staff

A __treble__ clef and a staff together make a treble *staff*.

Trace the brace and line.

G line

Trace. —○— Middle C

I'm in the treble staff.

F line

I'm in the bass staff.

The grand staff

A __bass__ clef and a staff together make a bass *staff*.

The grand staff is for low notes *and* high notes.

Name the colored keys.

Middle C

F   C   G

__bass__ __staff__ ← Treble staff or bass staff?

__treble__ __staff__ ← Treble staff or bass staff?

The grand staff is for __low__ notes *and* __high__ notes.

Middle C is between the bass and treble staffs.

Trace.

Color the G line green.

Color the F line yellow.

Complete this one by yourself.

Trace the brace and line too.

Middle C has 2 Neighbors.

9

Bubble.

Drip.

The lower neighbor is **B**. It looks like a floating **B**ubble.

B C D

The higher neighbor is **D**. It looks like a **D**rip waiting to fall.

D hangs below the treble staff, like a __drip__ waiting to fall.
B is on top of the bass staff, like a __bubble__ floating on water.

Trace. Draw lines to the keyboard.

D for Drip

B for Bubble

Middle C is singing in the shower.

Trace the clefs. Write the notes.

Trace the notes. Circle the correct words and arrows.

B   C   D   B

Step Skip ↑↓   Step Skip ↑↓   Step Skip ↑↓

O B

Doctor Mozart Music Theory Workbook, Answers for Level 1 & OB. © MMVI, MMXVII Machiko and Paul Christopher Musgrave.   Published by April Avenue Music.   www.DoctorMozart.com

The F Clef and G Clef

Why is the bass clef also called the F clef?

The bass clef has dots above and below the F line.

And it looks like a letter F.

It reminds us where F is.

F Line

The bass clef has dots above and below the __F__ line

What is another name for the bass clef?
___F clef___ What alphabet letter
does the bass clef look like? __F__
Name the fourth line in the bass staff: __F__

Why is the treble clef also called the G clef?

The treble clef curls around the G line.

It looks like a letter G,

and it reminds us where G is.

G Line

The treble clef curls around the __G__ line

What is another name for the treble clef?
___G clef___ What alphabet letter
does the treble clef look like? __G__
Name the second line in the treble staff? __G__

Trace the notes. Name them.

F   G

Trace the lines. →

Name the notes.

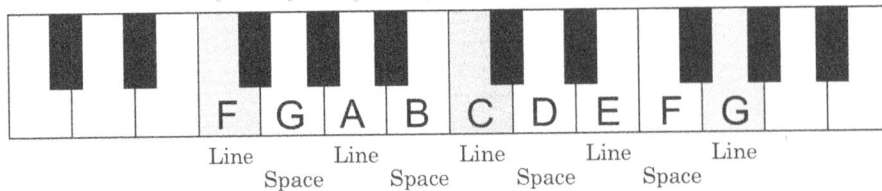

| F | G | A | B | C | D | E | F | G |

Line   Line   Line   Line   Line
    Space   Space   Space   Space

Measures and Bar Lines

Trace the bar lines.

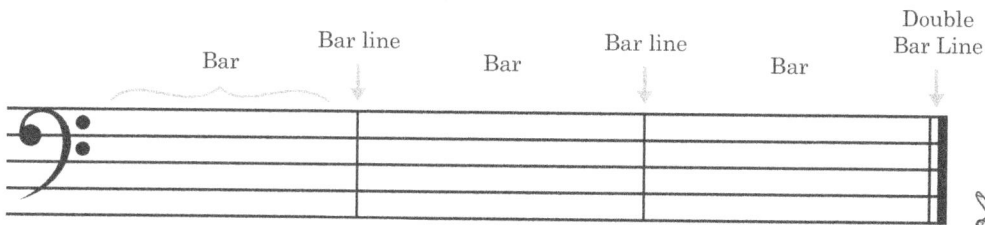

A double bar line is written at the very end of the music.

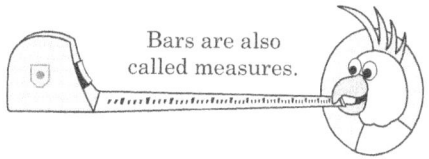

Bar   Bar line   Bar   Bar line   Bar   Double Bar Line

Bars are also called measures.

The area between two bar lines is called a __bar__. Bars are separated from each other by __bar__ lines. Bars are also called *measures*. Another word for *bar* is __measure__.

This is a repeat sign. It has two lines and two dots.

Repeat Sign

At the very end of the music, we write a __double__ bar line. A __repeat__ sign tells you to repeat the music. Another word for *measure* is __bar__.

Draw lines to match the words with the signs.

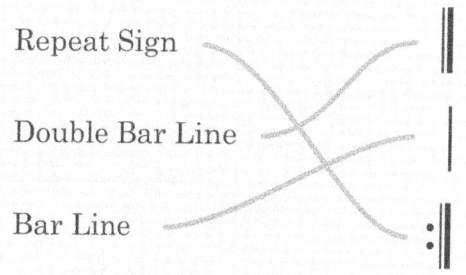

Repeat Sign

Double Bar Line

Bar Line

Bars are like fields. And bar *lines* are like fences.

Below, trace everything printed in gray. Write the word **bar** above each measure.

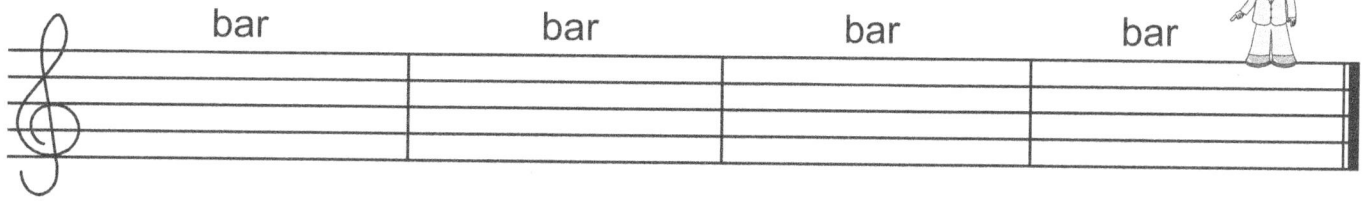

OB

bar   bar   bar   bar

Doctor Mozart Music Theory Workbook, Answers for Level 1 & OB. © MMVI, MMXVII Machiko and Paul Christopher Musgrave. Published by April Avenue Music. www.DoctorMozart.com

Quarter, Half, and Whole Notes

Quarter notes go at a medium walking speed. They get just **one beat** each.
What kind of note do you see at left? A ___quarter___ note.

How many beats does each quarter note usually get? _1_
Quarter notes are like the steps you take when you ___walk___.

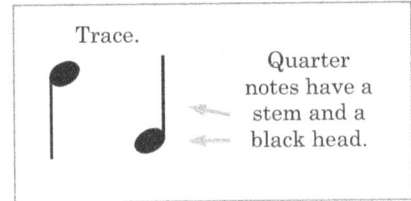

Trace. Quarter notes have a stem and a black head.

Trace the head first, then the stem.

Half notes go slower, like slow skating. They get **two beats** each.
What kind of note do you see at left? ___half___ note.

How many beats does each half note usually get? _2_
Half notes are slower, like slow ___skating___.

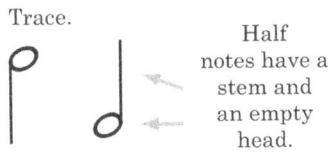

Trace. Half notes have a stem and an empty head.

One **whole note** is as long as two half notes.

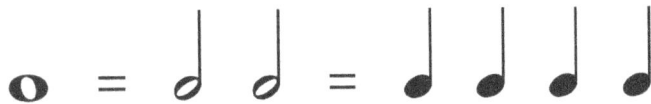

Trace. Whole notes have an empty head and no stem.

1 whole note is as long as _2_ half notes, or _4_ quarter notes.

4 ___quarter___ notes are as long as 2 ___half___ notes,
or 1 ___whole___ note.

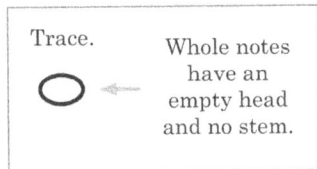

How many quarter notes are these notes equal to?

o = 4   ♩ = 2

How many quarter notes?

♩ + ♩ = 4

♩ + ♩ = 3

Doctor Mozart Music Theory Workbook, Answers for Level 1 & OB.   © MMVI, MMXVII Machiko and Paul Christopher Musgrave.   Published by April Avenue Music.   www.DoctorMozart.com

Chocolate Time

If two people share a chocolate bar, then each person can get half.
If two people share, how much can each person get?
__half__

In music, longer notes don't get more chocolate. Instead, they get more **time**.
Long notes get more __time__.

How Friends Share Chocolate

If your friends don't want any, you can keep the **whole** chocolate bar. This whole chocolate bar has 4 pieces.

If your friends don't want any, you can have the __whole__ chocolate bar.

If two people share, then each person gets **half** of the bar.

If two people share, each person gets __half__ (2 pieces each).

If four people share, then each person gets **one quarter**.

If four people share, each person gets __one quarter__ (1 piece).

How Notes Share Time

Whole notes don't share. One whole note gets **4 beats**, which is enough to fill a whole bar.

Trace the note. O

Number the squares. → | 1 | 2 | 3 | 4 |

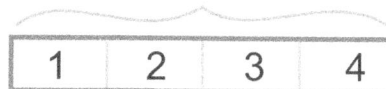

Each whole note gets __4__ beats.

These **half notes** get **2 beats** each.

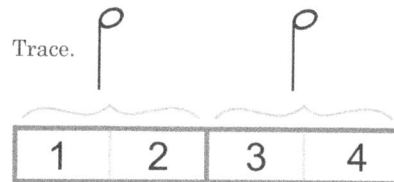

Trace.

Number the squares. | 1 | 2 | 3 | 4 |

Half notes get __2__ beats each.
How many half notes can fit in this bar? __2__

Quarter notes get only **1 beat** each.

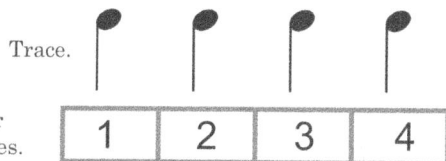

Trace.

Number the squares. | 1 | 2 | 3 | 4 |

Quarter notes get __1__ beat each.
How many of them can fit in this bar? __4__

O B

Stem Up or Stem Down?

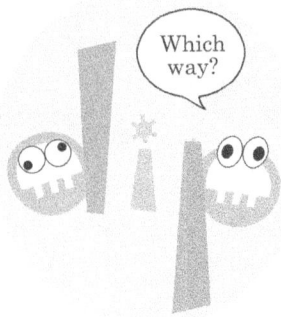

Which way?

dip

These notes are **below** the middle line, so the stem goes **up**.

These notes are **on** the middle line, so the stem can go **up or down.**

These notes are **above** the middle line, so the stems go **down**.

Middle Line

Trace the notes

Each of these notes look like a letter **d**.

Each of these notes look like a letter **p**.

A note should look like a letter **d** or **p**. Remember the word **dip**.
A note should *never* look like a letter b or q.

Which way should the stem go if the note is

below the middle line? ___Up___
on the middle line? ___Up or down___
above the middle line? ___Down___

Circle the alphabet letters that notes can look like:

(d) (p) b q

What word can help you remember this? __dip__

Draw stems on these notes.

This stem can also go up.

Trace these notes.

Quarter note

Stem. →
Filled-in head. →

Half note

← Stem.
← Empty head.

Whole note

← *No* stem.
← Empty head.

Write some quarter, half, and whole notes on various lines and spaces.

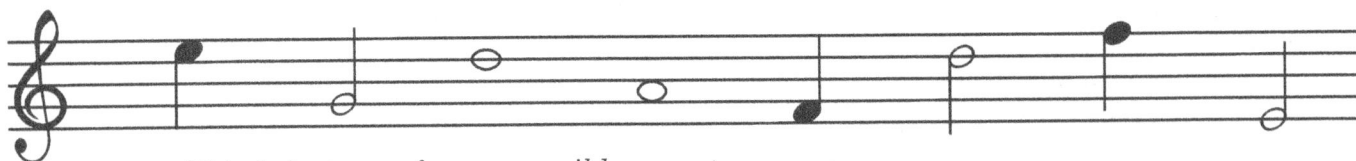

This is just one of many possible correct answers.

Doctor Mozart Music Theory Workbook, Answers for Level 1 & OB.   © MMVI, MMXVII Machiko and Paul Christopher Musgrave.   Published by April Avenue Music.   www.DoctorMozart.com

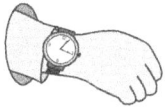

What is a Time Signature?

These are time signatures. Trace them.
Then write them by yourself, at the arrows.

Trace   Copy

What do time signatures tell us?

3
3 beats per bar.

4
Each beat is as long as a quarter note.

This 3 on the top tells you that there are __3__ beats in each bar. You should count 1, 2, 3, 1, 2, 3.

This 4 on the bottom tells you that each beat is a __quarter__ note in length.

Write an X under any bar that has too many or too few beats.

X   X

2
2 beats per bar.

2
Each beat is as long as a half note.

This 2 on the top tells you that there are __2__ beats in each bar. You should count 1, 2, 1, 2.

This 2 on the bottom tells you that each beat is a __half__ note in length.

O
B

Number the beats. Complete the time signatures.

1   2   3   4   1   2   1   2   3

* Two bar lines come before a time signature change.

Rhythm EXERCISE

Number the beats. Tap the half notes and quarter notes at the same time. Repeat until perfect.

Tap your **right hand** like the big feet stepping slowly.

Tap your **left hand** like the little feet, which step twice as fast.

1 2 3 4   1 2 3 4   1 2 3 4

Complete each time signature. Fill the empty bars with notes. Number the beats.

This is just one of many possible correct answers.

1 2 3 4   1 2 3 4   1 2 3   1 2 3

1 2   1 2   1 2 3 4   1 2 3 4

Complete each time signature. Tap, hands together. Repeat until perfect.

Doctor Mozart Music Theory Workbook, Answers for Level 1 & OB. © MMVI, MMXVII Machiko and Paul Christopher Musgrave.   Published by April Avenue Music.   www.DoctorMozart.com

Meet the Space Note Cs

Trace the notes. Name them.

Number the spaces

4
3
2
1

4
3
2
1

Draw lines.

Name the staff notes on the keyboard.

C
Space

F
Line

B
Line

C D

G
Line

C
Space

The low C is on the __2__ nd space

The high C is on the __3__ rd space.

Trace the notes.

Draw lines.

Name the staff notes on the keyboard.

C D E F G A B C D E F G A B C
Space · · · · · · · Line · · · · · · · Space

Write a note for each colored key.

Draw lines.

Name the colored keys.

C
Space

E
Space

G
Space

C
Line

E
Line

G
Line

C
Space

O
B

What 3 letter names do these colored keys have? __C E G__

Doctor Mozart Music Theory Workbook, Answers for Level 1 & OB.   © MMVI, MMXVII Machiko and Paul Christopher Musgrave.   Published by April Avenue Music.   www.DoctorMozart.com

What is a Chord?

This is a chord. Say it like this: "kord".

A chord is a group of special notes played together.
Here are two C chords.

Each C chord has 3 notes: C, E, & G.

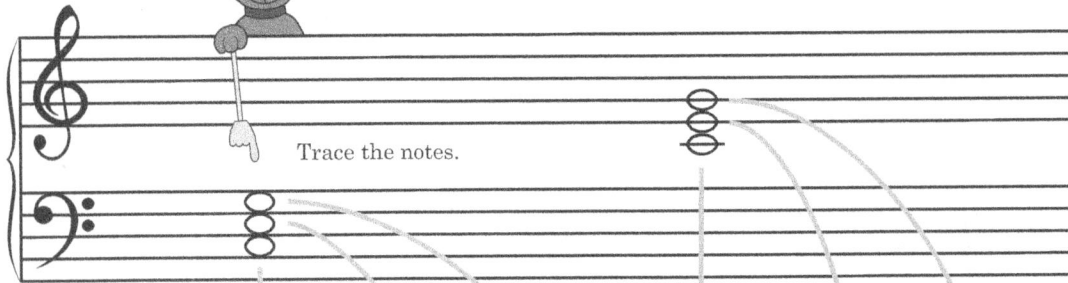

Trace the notes.

Trace the lines.

Name the colored keys.

C   E   G   C   E   G

Space   Space   Space   Line   Line   Line

In each of these two chords, the lowest note is __C__.
A group of special notes played together is called a __chord__.

Write a C chord in each staff.

C chord

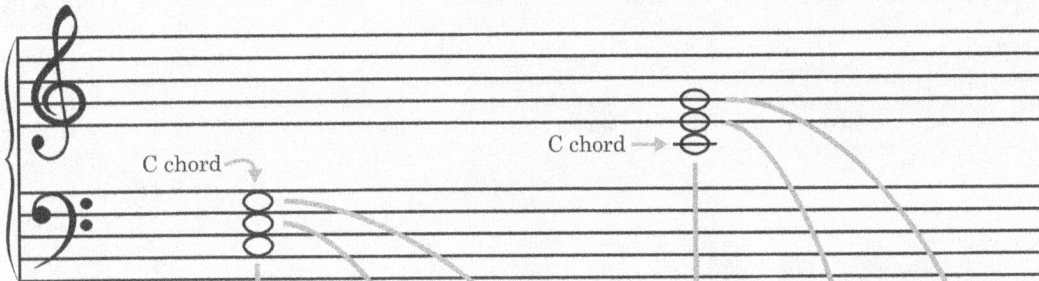

C chord

C chord

Draw lines.

Name the C chord notes.

C   E   G   C   E   G

Space   Line

These C chords have only *space* notes in the bass staff, and only __line__ notes in the treble staff.

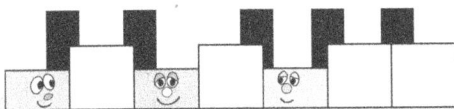

What 3 notes belong in a C chord? __C E G__

Next, circle the C chords.

Doctor Mozart Music Theory Workbook, Answers for Level 1 & OB. © MMVI, MMXVII Machiko and Paul Christopher Musgrave.   Published by April Avenue Music.   www.DoctorMozart.com

StaFF Quiz

Draw note stems.
Circle the correct words and arrows.

Step	Step	**Step**	**Step**	**Step**	Step	Step	Step
Skip	Skip	Skip	Skip	Skip	**Skip**	**Skip**	**Skip**
↑↓	↑↓	↑↓	↑↓	↑↓	↑↓	↑↓	↑↓

Write a C chord on each staff. Is the treble staff C chord made with line notes? __Yes__

Draw lines.

Name the keys
that belong to
each C chord.

C   E   G   C   E   G

Draw lines from notes to keys. Name the notes.

C   F   B C D   G   C

O
B

Next, write all the notes between the two space note Cs. Name all the notes.

C D E F G A B C   C D E F G A B C

Expert Exam

Add the beats.

♩ + ♩ = 3
2   1

♩ + ♩ + ♩ + o = 8
1   2   1   4

♩ + o + ♩ = 7
1   4   2

♩ + ♩ = 4
2   2

After each printed note, write a neighboring note. Follow the arrows.

Trace.

Name the notes.

C D F G B C   D C G F C B

Step ↑   Step ↑   Step ↑   Step ↓   Step ↓   Step ↓

Next, look at how each note is named.
Then write the correct clef on each staff.

E   C   D   B

C   C   A   C

B   B   A   A

Treble Staff Elephants

This elephant knows how to remember the treble staff line notes.

Feet — F
Dirty — D
Big — B
Got — G
Elephants — E

Trace the lines

Name the colored keys.

C E G B D F

The sentence *Elephants Got Big Dirty Feet* helps us remember the treble staff __line__ notes.

Fill in the blanks: Elephants Got **Big** Dirty **Feet**.

Name these treble staff notes.

Draw lines.

C E G B D F

C E G B D F

Write a line note for each letter.

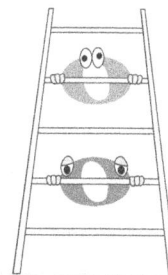

E F G D B

Always start each staff with a clef. If a gray clef is already printed, trace it.

After each printed note, write a note that is one step higher.

One step higher.

E F G A B C D E F G

Name the notes.

O B

FACE for Space Notes

The treble staff space notes spell FACE.

The word __FACE__ can help you remember the treble staff space notes.

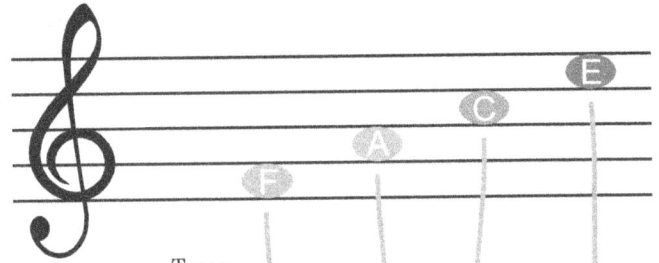

Trace.

Name the colored keys.

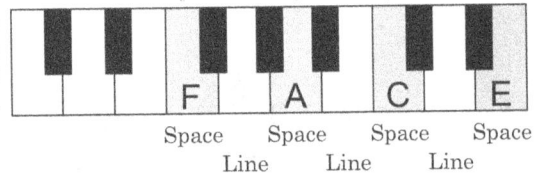

F A C E

Space Space Space Space
Line   Line   Line

Space notes cannot be neighbors, because there are ___line___ notes between them.

Name these treble staff notes.

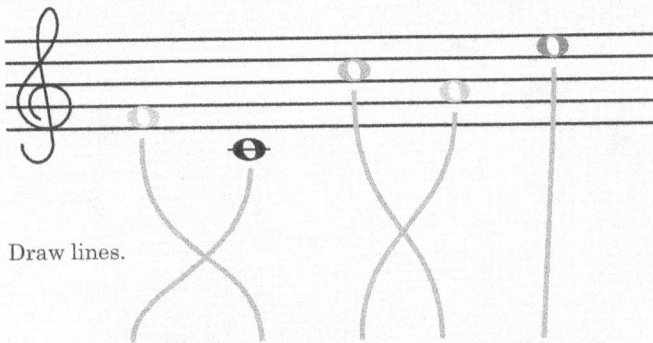

Draw lines.

C F A C E

C F A C E

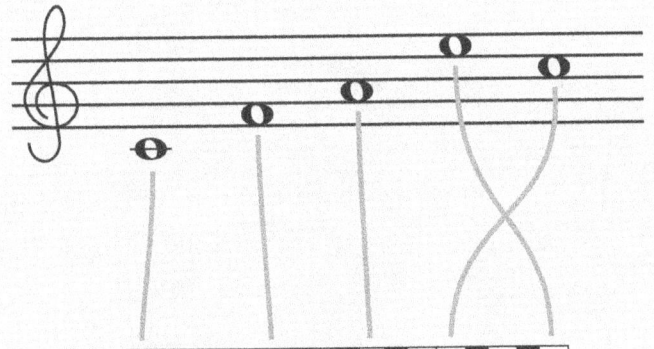

After each printed note, write a note that is one step lower.

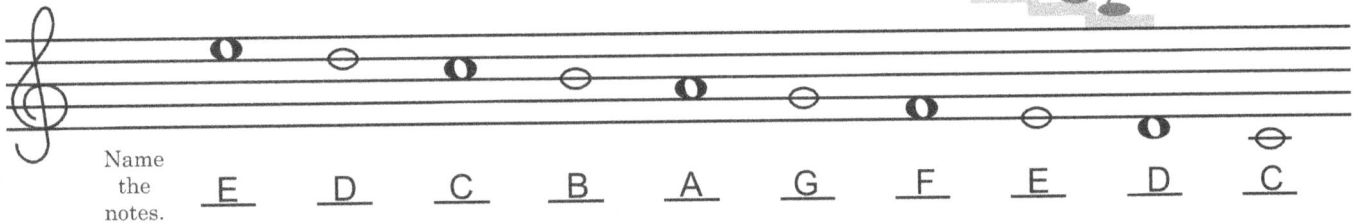

Name the notes.   E D C B A G F E D C

Draw a treble clef. Name the notes.

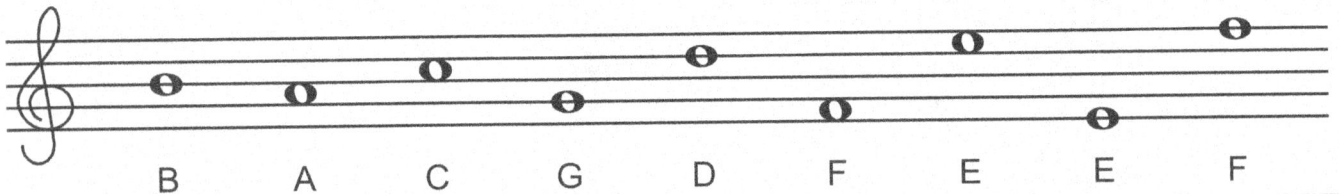

B A C G D F E E F

Great Big Dogs in the Bass Staff

This great big dog knows how to remember the bass staff line notes.

Great **Big** Dogs **Fight** Animals.

Animals
Fight
Dogs
Big
Great

Trace.

Name the colored keys.

G   B   D   F   A

Complete the sentence: Great **Big**
Dogs **Fight**   **Animals**   .

This sentence can help you remember the bass staff ___line___ notes.

Name these bass staff notes.

G   B   D   F   A

G   B   D   F   A

Write a line note for each letter.

F   G   A   B   D

After each printed note, write a note that is one step higher.

G   A   B   C   D   E   F   G   A   B

Name the notes.

Doctor Mozart Music Theory Workbook, Answers for Level 1 & OB. © MMVI, MMXVII Machiko and Paul Christopher Musgrave.   Published by April Avenue Music.   www.DoctorMozart.com

O
B

What Do Cows Eat?

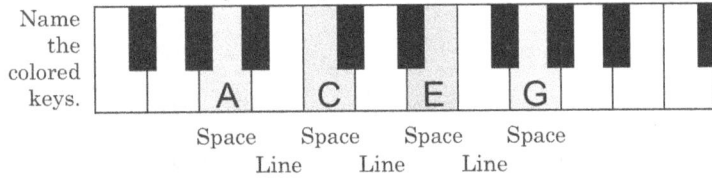

This cow knows how to remember the bass staff space notes.

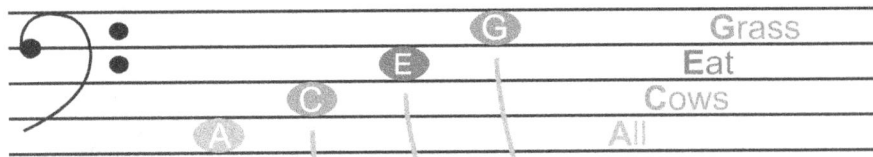

Grass
Eat
Cows
All

Trace.

Name the colored keys.

A   C   E   G

Space   Space   Space   Space
Line   Line   Line

Fill in the blanks:
All __Cows__ Eat __Grass__.

Space notes cannot be neighbors, because there are __line__ notes between them.

Name these bass staff notes.

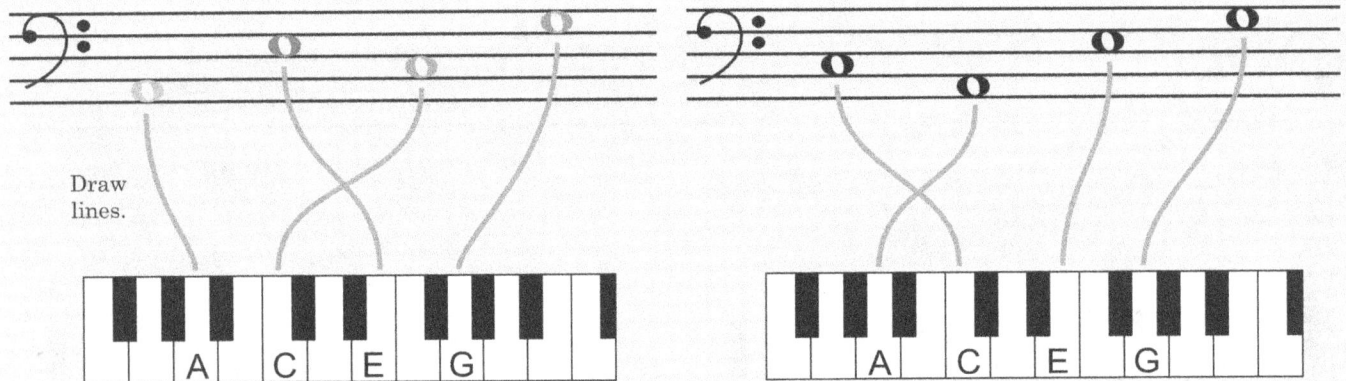

Draw lines.

A   C   E   G   A   C   E   G

After each printed note, write a note that is one step lower.

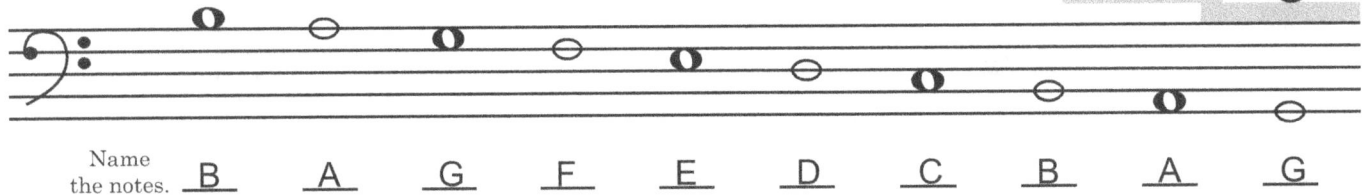

Name the notes. __B__ __A__ __G__ __F__ __E__ __D__ __C__ __B__ __A__ __G__

Write a bass clef. Name the notes.

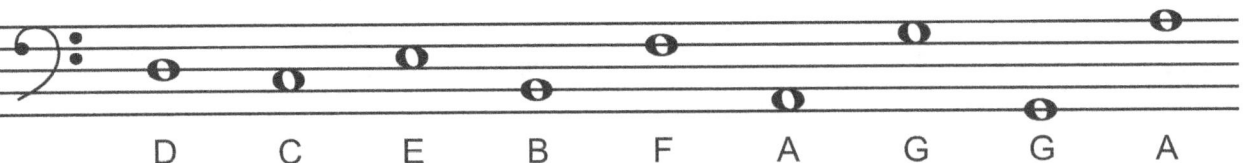

D   C   E   B   F   A   G   G   A

Doctor Mozart Music Theory Workbook, Answers for Level 1 & OB. © MMVI, MMXVII Machiko and Paul Christopher Musgrave. Published by April Avenue Music. www.DoctorMozart.com

Treble Staff Giraffe

There are 2 Gs in the treble staff. The high G is named after me.

Drip, face, and giraffe.

G — G for **G**iraffe

G — G Line

Trace.

Name the treble staff space notes.

D F G A C E G

Line   Space

Name these treble staff notes.

Draw lines.

D F G   C E G

D F G A   E G

Name these treble staff notes.

C   C   D   D   E   E   F   F   G   G

These alphabet characters show the name of each note. Write the correct clef on each staff.

A   F   B   G   C   E

O
B

Doctor Mozart Music Theory Workbook. Answers for Level 1 & OB. © MMVI, MMXVII Machiko and Paul Christopher Musgrave.   Published by April Avenue Music.   www.DoctorMozart.com

Mr. Bass Staff Foot

Foot, cows, bubble.

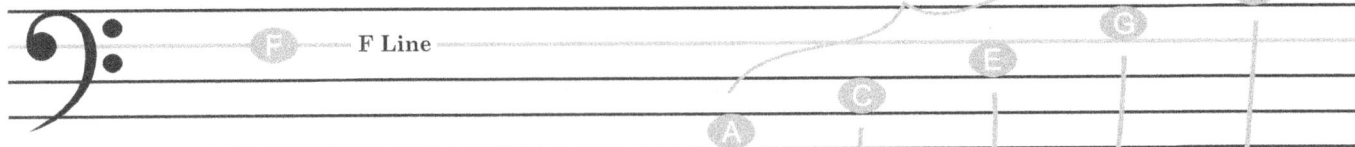

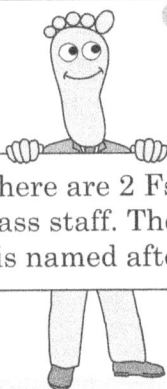

F Line

F for Foot

There are 2 Fs in the bass staff. The low F is named after me.

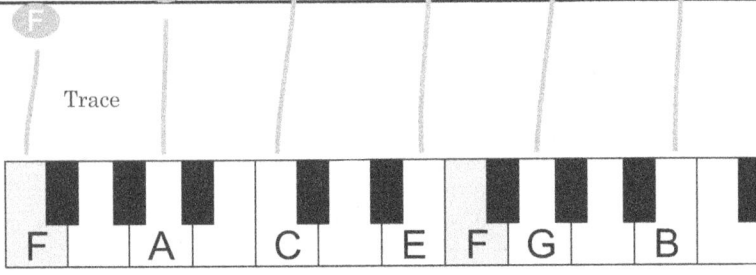

Trace

Space

Name the space notes.

Line

F   A   C   E   F   G   B

Name these bass staff notes.

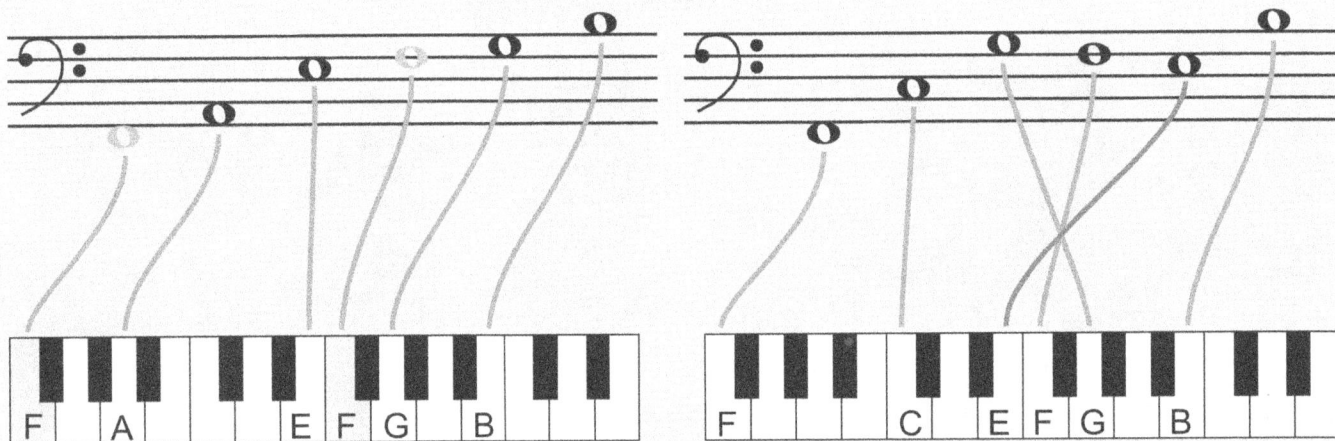

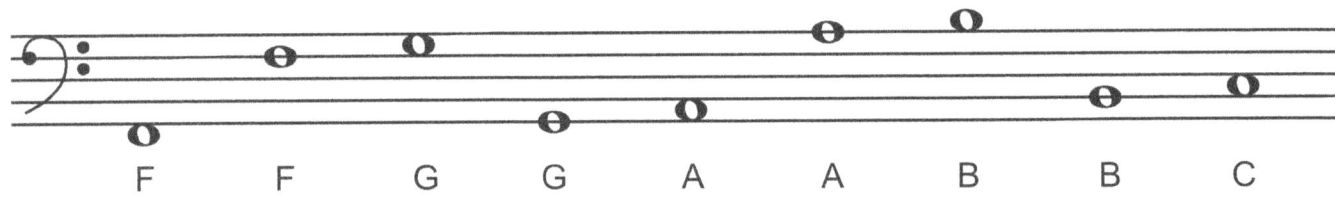

F   A   E   F   G   B

F   C   E   F   G   B

Name these bass staff notes.

F   F   G   G   A   A   B   B   C

Write the correct clef on each staff.

Drip FACE Giraffe Elephants

Here are all the treble staff notes you have learned.

Feet
Dirty
Big
Got
Elephants

E
C
A
F

Draw lines.

Name the notes.

C D E F G A B C D E F G

Name these treble staff notes.

Draw lines.

D E F G A B C D E F G

Name these treble staff notes.

G D E F F E B D G

Draw a treble clef. Write the notes.

Got Big Dirty Elephants Feet Drip Giraffe

O
B

Foot Cows Bubble Dogs

Here are all the bass staff notes you have learned.

Animals
Fight
Dogs
Big
Great

Grass
Eat
Cows
All

Draw lines.

Name the notes.

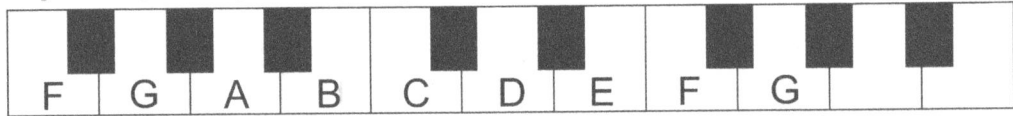

F G A B C D E F G A B

A B C D E F G

Name these bass staff notes.

Draw lines.

Name the notes.

F G A B C D E F G

Name these bass staff notes.

B F G A A G D F B

Draw a bass clef. Write the notes.

Grass   Dogs   Big   Animals   Cows   Foot   Bubble

Doctor Mozart Music Theory Workbook, Answers for Level 1 & OB. © MMVI, MMXVII Machiko and Paul Christopher Musgrave.   Published by April Avenue Music.   www.DoctorMozart.com

Treble & Bass Quiz

Name these treble staff notes.

C C D D E E F F G G

Draw a treble clef. Write two notes for each letter, as shown above.

C C D D E E F F G G

What are the red arrows pointing at?

Bar line   Double bar line   Repeat sign

Name these bass staff notes.

F F G G A A B B C C

Draw a bass clef.
Write two notes for each
letter, as shown above.

Bass Trio

F F G G A A B B C C

OB

Tap each rhythm, hands together.
Repeat until perfect.

Write your own rhythm. Tap it too!

This is just one of many possible correct answers.

Write your own rhythm.

This is just one of many possible correct answers.

Tap it!

Write a single note in each blank.

Add the beats.

Quarter Rests

  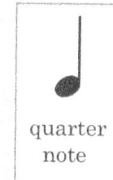

These are the same length.

quarter rest

quarter note

When you talk, you hear your voice. But as you take a breath, your voice is silent. Music has silences too. We write them with special signs called **rests**.

A silence in music is called a __rest__ .

A quarter rest is as long as a __quarter__ note.

Next, answer with a single note that has the same time value.

𝄽 = ♩   𝄽 + 𝄽 = ♩   𝄽 + 𝄽 + 𝄽 + 𝄽 = 𝅝

A quarter rest looks like a zig-zag above a curl. Trace these quarter rests. Then write 3 more.

You can start from the top or the bottom.

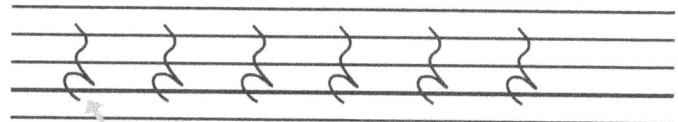

Curl around the 2nd line.

Number the beats. Write quarter rests for any missing beats.

1 2 3 4   1 2 3 4   1 2 3   1 2 3

Add the quarter note beats.

♩ + 𝄽 = ☐ 2
1   1

♩ + 𝄽 + ♩ = ☐ 4
2   1   1

𝅝 − 𝄽 = ☐ 3
4   1

♩ − 𝄽 = ☐ 1
2   1

OB

Doctor Mozart Music Theory Workbook, Answers for Level 1 & OB.   © MMVI, MMXVII Machiko and Paul Christopher Musgrave.   Published by April Avenue Music.   www.DoctorMozart.com

Half Rests

Same length.

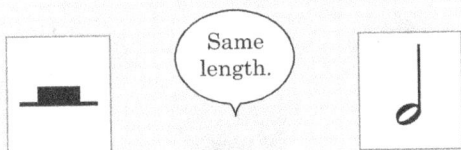

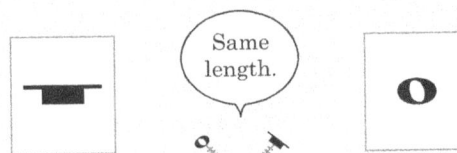

Trace and draw 3 more.

3rd space

Whole Rests

Same length.

Trace and draw 3 more.

A half rest looks like a hat.

Whole rests and half rests are both written in the __3__rd space. Write the rests shown.

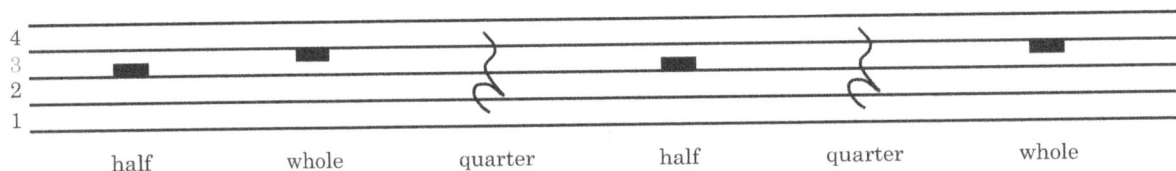

half   whole   quarter   half   quarter   whole

Write rests that have the number of beats shown.

Example

1   2

2   1   4   1   2   4

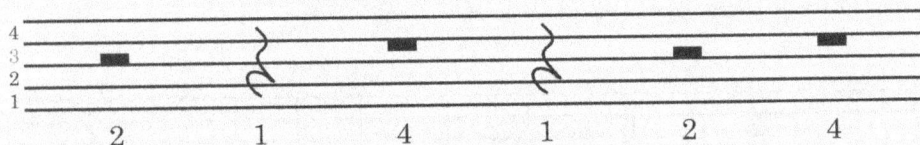

A whole rest looks like a hole in the ground.

Add the quarter note beats.

$\quad + \quad + \quad = \boxed{7}$

Two quarter rests equal one half rest.

$\quad - \quad = \boxed{1}$

$\quad + \quad + \quad = \boxed{9}$

$\quad + \quad + \quad = \boxed{4}$

$\quad - \quad = \boxed{2}$

Notes & Clefs

Name the notes.

F F F F G G G G A A A B B B C C C

B F D G G A F E A G E F D B

Look at how each note is named.
Then write the correct clef
at the beginning of each staff.

G   E   F   A

G   G   E   E

F   D   D   F

O
B

Accent Your Music

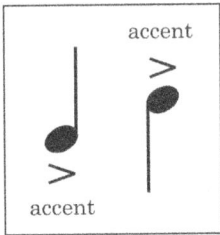

Trace the accents at left (>). If a note has an accent mark, you should play it louder.

Accented notes should be played __louder__.

Next, draw note stems and bar lines. Write an accent on the first note of each bar. Name the notes.

accent

accent

G B F A C A G D B E

Crescendo and Diminuendo

Crescendo means gradually get louder. *Diminuendo* means gradually get softer.
Here are the musical signs:

Kre-SHEN-doe

Dim-in-u-EN-do

crescendo

diminuendo (or decrescendo)

__crescendo__ means gradually get louder. __diminuendo__ means gradually get softer.

Draw lines to match each term with its meaning.

crescendo (cresc.) — Play gradually more softly.

decrescendo (or decresc.) — Play gradually louder.

diminuendo (or dim.) —

accent — Play the note louder.

Number the beats. Draw bar lines. Write some cresc. and dim. signs.

Trace.

(Example answer)

1 2 3 4 1 2 3 4 1 2 3 4 1 2 3 4

Trace

Number

Draw

Dynamics Marks

Fill in the blanks. Trace the arrows.

pp

pp = pianissimo

Play or sing very softly.

Pianissimo = *pp*

p

p = piano

Play or sing softly.

Piano = *p*

mp

mp = mezzo piano

Medium quiet, a little louder than *piano*.

Mezzo piano = *mp*

mf

mf = mezzo forte

Medium loud, a little louder than mezzo piano.

Mezzo forte = *mf*

f

f = forte

Play or sing loudly.

Forte = *f*

Signs that tell you how soft or loud to play are called dynamics marks.

ff

ff = fortissimo

Play or sing very loudly.

Fortissimo = *ff*

Number these dynamics marks, from 1 for the quietest, to 6 for the loudest.

p	*mp*	*mf*	*ff*	*pp*	*f*
2	3	4	6	1	5

Signs that tell you how soft or loud to play are called _____dynamics_____ marks.

O B

Staccato

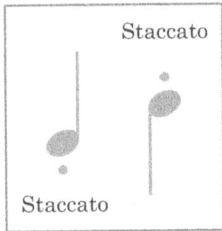

At left, the dots make the notes staccato. Let go of staccato notes immediately after you play them. If a note has a staccato mark, you should let go ___**immediately**___.

Next, draw stems and bar lines. Then find an empty space near each note head, and write a dot in it.

Staccato

Staccato

Trace.

Name the notes. **F** **A** **B** **E** **G** **C** **A** **C**

Legato

Trace the slurs.

slur

slur

Trace the slurs at left. A slur tells you to play **legato**, which means *join* the notes as you play them. Legato is the opposite of staccato.

The opposite of staccato is ___**legato**___.

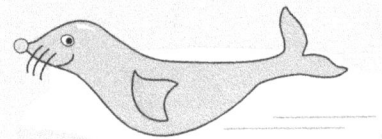

Marks that tell you whether to play staccato or legato are called **articulation marks**. Staccato and legato marks are called ___**articulation**___ marks.

Fermata Molto Poco

The fermata sign tells you to pause on a note or a rest.

Trace.

fermata

Molto means very much.

Molto allegro means very fast.

Poco means a little.

Poco a poco means gradually.

Write the correct terms.   A little ___**poco**___   Very much ___**molto**___   Pause ___**fermata**___

Doctor Mozart Music Theory Workbook, Answers for Level 1 & OB. © MMVI, MMXVII Machiko and Paul Christopher Musgrave.   Published by April Avenue Music.   www.DoctorMozart.com

Dynamics & Articulation Quiz

Draw a line from each *sign* to its *name*, and then to its *meaning*.

Fortissimo Trio

Pianissimo
ᴾᴾ Recital ᴾᴾ

Sign	Name	Meaning
♩ >	piano	Play the note louder
p	accent	Soft
ff	fortissimo	Very loud
	pianissimo	Very soft
pp	diminuendo (dim.) or decrescendo (decresc.)	Gradually get softer
	forte	Gradually get louder
f	crescendo (cresc.)	Loud
mf	mezzo piano	A little louder than *p*
mp	mezzo forte	A little louder than *mp*
	fermata	Let go of the note immediately
	staccato	Pause

Next, name what each blue arrow is pointing to.

accent   staccato   slur   diminuendo or decrescendo   fermata

mp   crescendo   *mf*   bar line   *pp*   repeat sign

mezzo piano   crescendo   mezzo forte   pianissimo   repeat sign

O B

Musical Review

Tap these rhythms. Repeat until perfect.

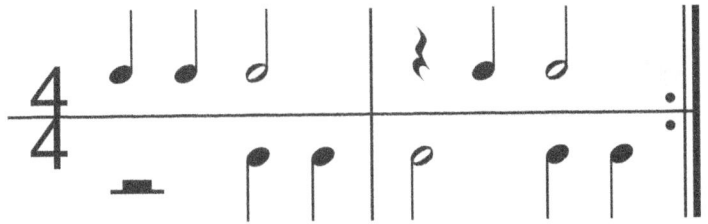

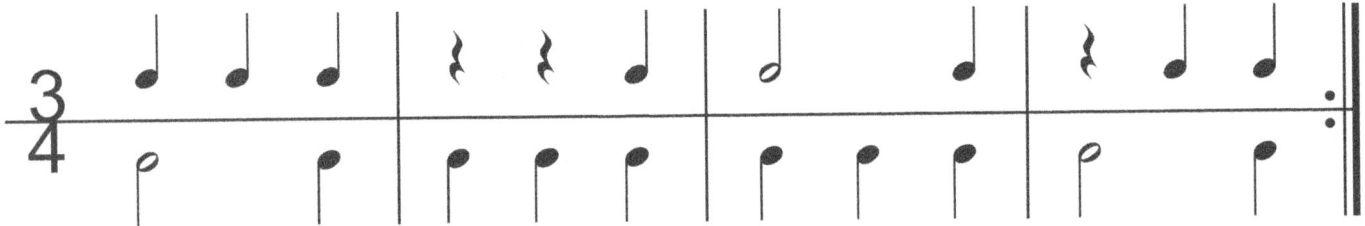

Draw lines to the right answers.

(cow)	How to remember the bass staff line notes.
(dog)	How to remember the bass staff space notes.
(food bowl)	poco
(food bowl)	molto
(seal)	staccato
(seal)	legato or slurred

(dog with bubble)	D for drip
(faucet drip)	B for bubble
(elephant)	The treble staff space notes spell FACE.
(man)	How to remember the treble staff line notes.
(dog with calculator)	A quarter note looks like d or p.
(bowl)	fermata